William Allen Butler

Mrs. Limber's raffle

A church fair and its victims

William Allen Butler

Mrs. Limber's raffle
A church fair and its victims

ISBN/EAN: 9783743302907

Manufactured in Europe, USA, Canada, Australia, Japa

Cover: Foto ©Thomas Meinert / pixelio.de

Manufactured and distributed by brebook publishing software
(www.brebook.com)

William Allen Butler

Mrs. Limber's raffle

MRS. LIMBER'S RAFFLE

OR, A CHURCH FAIR AND ITS VICTIMS

A SHORT STORY

BY

WILLIAM ALLEN BUTLER

NEW EDITION

NEW YORK
D. APPLETON AND COMPANY
1894

PREFACE.

THE narrative of Mrs. Limber's experience in the management of a church-fair raffle, as contained in the following pages, was published in 1876, anonymously, in order that the moral which it sought to enforce might stand on its own merits, free from any element, either of strength or weakness, attaching to personal advocacy. The book was widely circulated, and its condemnation of raffling was not met by any adverse criticism or answered by any opposing argument. A new edition of the story being called for, its authorship is avowed; and attention may fitly be called to the great advance in sound public opinion on the subject of lotteries, during the eighteen years which have elapsed since its first publication. The scandalous attempt in Louisiana in 1890 to perpetuate, on an enormous scale, a lottery system for the benefit of the State, with the intent of drawing its resources from the entire country, aroused a storm of indignation which swept away its local supports, and fastened a brand of outlawry on an evil which is now denounced and prohibited by the Constitution of almost every State in the Union.

Raffling, which is included in the prohibition, still survives and flourishes, for the reason that the public conscience, while awakened to the evils of gambling on a large scale and in its grosser forms, winks at the same evil in its lesser proportions, partly as a peccadillo and partly from its serviceableness as an ally of benevolence—a bad means sanctified by a good end. The sympathies of charitable women, especially, repel the idea of wrong or immorality as inhering in anything which stimulates the impulse of benevolence by the added zest of chance; and accordingly they set aside the mandate of the law and the moral principle on which it rests, with a charming indifference to both, characteristic of their sex, which shrinks instinctively from impurity and evil, but smilingly chaperones a seemingly innocent vice which not only leans to virtue's side, but is obtrusively active in her service. Truth, thus wounded in the house of her friends, finds few defenders in the ranks of those whose special duty should be the education of the conscience and the conservation of morals. This result is largely due to the inherent difficulty of asserting a moral principle which depends for its true acceptance upon a process of reasoning, and also to the ungraciousness of discouraging the efforts of well-meaning and benevolent people. Meanwhile the demoralization goes on; boys and girls make their first essay in gambling by drawing some petty prize in the chances of a raffle; and the general assent of the community is easily enlisted, on the plea of philanthropy or Christian charity, in aid of deliberate violations of a positive law and an established moral principle.

WILLIAM ALLEN BUTLER.

ROUND OAK, YONKERS, N. Y., *May, 1894.*

CONTENTS.

MRS. LIMBER'S RAFFLE.

CHAPTER I.

ST. PARVUS BY MOONLIGHT.

MRS. DAVID LIMBER was a housekeeper without fear and without reproach. There was but one key to her storeroom, and she held it with a firm hand. She was an active manager, with a keen eye for dirt, a quick ear for all unlicensed sounds, and a sense of smell almost supernatural. Her good bargains were proverbial, and she was a standard authority on butter. No one could excel her in that gift of domestic divination, by which experienced housewives can announce, at the first sound of the streetdoor bell, who is ringing it, and can detect the existence of "something burning," or of unfastened windows, or suspicious footfalls in distant corners of the house, at the dead of night, in spite of all adverse presumptions, or of the criminal indifference or apathy of husbands.

Among other high prerogatives of Mrs. Limber, was that of being, as she was in the habit of expressing it, "the last one up in the house," by which it is to be understood, not that she rose in the morning after every one else, but that she did not retire at night until the whole family was actually or constructively in bed.

In the enjoyment of this privilege, Mrs. Limber was seated, one Saturday evening, in her little up-stairs sitting-room, in the absence of her husband, the only person in her spacious mansion who had not ended the week's work or play and gone to bed. A hickory-fire, which the first October frost had made a cheerful novelty on her hearth, gave out a glow in harmony with her own genial presence. A large basket, piled with stockings, was placed conveniently by her side, and, as she plied her needle with the quick certainty of an expert in the art and mystery of darning, two unsolved enigmas occupied her thoughts—the first, where all the holes in the stockings came from; and the second, why no one could mend them but herself.

It was evident, however, that these questions were suggested by no bitterness of spirit, and that they would, if answered, have probably resulted in a quiet sense of satisfaction, on Mrs. Limber's part, that her husband and children were pushing their way in the world, and she was helping them do it, for her face wore a smile, and her heart was in her work as really, if not as literally, as her hand. Seen at this moment by even the most unskilled physiognomist, Mrs. Limber would have appeared the embodiment of good sense and good temper, a fair-faced, free-hearted matron, blessed with a contented husband and healthy children, and with a will and a way of her own. This is precisely what she was.

The hall-clock struck eleven. The clock in Mrs. Limber's bedroom did the same, and so did the clock on her sitting-room mantel-piece. What Charles V. found it impossible to do, Mrs. Limber had accomplished; her clocks struck together. At the last stroke she paused in her work, folded away the nineteenth stocking, one only out of ten pair having been wonderfully preserved from new rents, thanks to the strength of former darns, and laid it on the top of the pile, to which she gave a motherly pat with her broad, white palm. The final destination of this precious basket was the top of the bureau in her

own bedroom, but just now she let it rest on the
work-table at which she had been seated, while
she opened the window, with the single intent of
closing the outside blinds, according to her inva-
riable habit, and as an indispensable preliminary
to a quiet night's rest.

But this movement, so commonplace and me-
chanical, was changed into a gesture of surprise
and delight as the opened window disclosed a
scene in which the most familiar and ordinary
objects were clothed with a beauty as rare as it
was unexpected. The night was clear, and the
moon, at its full, was at that instant transform-
ing, by its magic touch, the prosaic manufacturing
village of Spindle, upon which David Limber's
front-windows looked down, and in which his
own factories were the most prominent objects,
into one of the selectest nooks of fairy-land. The
tall chimneys, the shingle roofs, the tinned cupo-
la of the court-house, the church-spires, the black
mass of railroad-buildings at the junction-depot—
all took on a new aspect, and the surrounding
hills and woods seemed for once in harmony with
the quiet town, which was, in reality and by daylight, one of the noisiest and most obtrusive county seats and railway centres which the genius
of modern improvement ever thrust into any

one of the many happy valleys of the Empire State.

Mrs. Limber's eye rested on the whole moon-lit scene. Although much more given to the practical than the ideal, she did not, at that witching hour, stop to think how much of it was owned in fee by her husband, and subject, by virtue of her tender relation to him, to her own inchoate right of dower. Her unselfish gaze turned from the clustered factory-roofs and lingered on the sleeping village, resting with special satisfaction on the cross-tipped spire of the little church of St. Parvus. Wooden though it was, and somewhat out of the line of a true perpendicular, it seemed to her a model of grace and proportion. The Grecian pediment of the First Presbyterian Church, it is true, was pure Parian in the moonlight; the square, brick tower of the Baptists, bathed in the silver sheen, was redeemed from its native ugliness; even the Methodist Meeting-House, touched by the lunar beam, wore a tint better than that for which it had long been awaiting the painter's brush; while the Roman Catholic Church, planted at a respectful distance, but on a commanding eminence, seemed to catch and reflect, on its large gilt cross, more than its share of the impartial

moonlight. But St. Parvus pierced the serene
sky with the tallest steeple, and soared heaven-
ward with a sense of conscious supremacy. So,
at least, it seemed to Mrs. Limber.

And yet, as she gave one last, loving glance,
and gently drew the blinds together, secured the
fastenings, turned the bolt of the sash, and then,
after her immemorial habit, made a spasmodic
effort to reopen the window, by way of making
assurance doubly sure, Mrs. Limber heaved a
sigh. This first sigh, like her last glance, was
given to St. Parvus, and was inspired by the
thought that, however bright its aspect by moonlight, its every-day condition was one of chronic
and desperate poverty, so desperate that Mr. Limber and his fellow-vestrymen were kept out of
their houses and their beds on this very Saturday
night to sit up with an incurable and exasperat-
ing church debt, and to devise ways and means to
be rid of it. No wonder it seemed to Mrs.
Limber as disagreeable and troublesome as the
strangled Hunchback in the "Arabian Nights,"
a dead weight, not to be concealed or disposed
of, with the fatal disadvantage of entire inability
to lay it at the door of any other church.

The utter indifference of the general population of Spindle, manufacturers, operatives and all,

to this pitiable condition of St. Parvus, was something which Mrs. Limber, to use her own language, "never did and never could comprehend." It confirmed her belief in the doctrine of total depravity that the superior privileges which were enjoyed at this exclusive shrine, on as favorable terms as those held out by any First or Second Presbyterian, any Wesleyan Methodist, any Freewill Baptist, or any Reformed Dutch Church, should attract so few adherents, while those rival societies were as strong in numbers and as easy in their finances as they were, according to Mrs. Limber's ideas, unsound in doctrine.

Equally incomprehensible, and not to be accounted for by any hypothesis, doctrinal or otherwise, was the way in which the worthy Rector of St. Parvus, the Rev. Alban Chancel, ignored and dismissed from consideration, as he might have done some pestilent heresy or petty scandal, the depleted state of the finances of his church, pursuing his weekly and daily round of ministerial duty with as much precision and with as comfortable a sense of parochial independence as if the revenues of Old Trinity had been at his sole disposal.

"Mr. Chancel hardly seems to know that there is such a thing as a church debt," Mrs. Limber

had said to the rector's wife, her bosom friend,
as they diverged, in conversation one day, from
the absorbing topics of dress and domestics to
the distresses of St. Parvus.

Mrs. Chancel was an invalid, but somewhat
skilled in repartee.

"Do you think, my dear, that if Mr. Chancel
were to borrow trouble the parish debt could be
paid any sooner?"

"No," said matter-of-fact Mrs. Limber; "but
he does not seem to take it much to heart. Now,
I always worry over a debt until it is paid."

"Oh, if this were Mr. Chancel's debt, I dare
say he would worry over it, but, instead of his
taking it to his heart, perhaps it would be as
well for the pew-holders to take it to their pock-
ets."

"Of course, the parish owes the debt," said
Mrs. Limber, and the discourse of the ladies
gravitated again toward the last item of domestic
experience.

But, if the good rector and his wife bore the
burden of the debt too lightly, it weighed heavi-
ly enough on the soul of Mrs. Limber, the most
faithful of his faithful flock. She was the cham-
pion, though after a strictly feminine, unhistoric,
and illogical fashion of her own, of the highest

ecclesiasticism, and delighted in her reputation as an uncompromising churchwoman, who stood for Episcopacy in general, and St. Parvus in particular, against all comers and all goers, as she would have stood for her husband and children, determined to do her whole duty even should she be left, like Dean Swift's dearly-beloved Roger, the sole auditor of the rector's exhortations.

Of all the many contributions made to St. Parvus by this estimable parishioner, the most valuable was David Limber himself, whom she had brought over, bodily—and he was a good two hundred pounds weight—from the First Presbyterian Church and Dr. Flatfoot. There had been a former Mrs. Limber who was Presbyterian. She died, in the fifth year of her married life, leaving a boy, three years old, and an infant daughter. Her husband, seven years later, had married again, with the full consent and approbation of every man, woman, and child, in Spindle, capable of forming and expressing an opinion on the subject. This unanimity of sentiment was partly owing to the fact that Mr. Limber's popularity was so great that, whatever he had chosen to do, short of marrying his grandmother, would have been presumptively right, but it was due even more to the real wisdom of his choice.

2

Everybody knew Martha Fleming, the only child of the old village doctor whose horse and chaise had stopped, at one time or another, at almost every door in the county before Spindle numbered a tithe of its present population, and whose professional repute, in spite of the inroads of younger practitioners, had continued to the day of his death. His daughter had kept his house for many years, tenderly caring for him in his declining days, and it was not until after his death that she would admit the idea of being more to any one else than she had been to him; but when at twenty-six she married David Limber, the leading manufacturer of the place, only fifteen years her senior, and by right entitled to as good a wife as Spindle, or the world at large, could afford, it was universally admitted, at all tea-tables and elsewhere, that she had done well and wisely. Not long after his second marriage, Mr. Limber, who during a sober courtship had been a constant attendant at St. Parvus, was seated punctually at the head of the pew which his departed father-in-law had occupied whenever his Sunday rounds permitted. With a little aid from his wife, the new recruit, who had privately expressed his fears that he was "rather stiff in the joints" for the services of St. Parvus, was in due time fully initiated as a churchman. He took kindly to the change, but showed symptoms of recusance when, at the end of a year, he found himself, on Easter Tuesday, suddenly metamorphosed into a warden.

"There is no warrant for it in Scripture," said he to the rector's wife, whom Mrs. Limber had called to her aid in overcoming his scruples. "There's a town clerk mentioned in the Acts, and a chamberlain, but never a warden or a vestryman."

"And where," said Mrs. Chancel, "is mention made of a trustee or a synod?"

This retort did not make his personal duty any clearer to Mr. Limber, but he yielded, at last, and soon ascertained that, whether warranted by Scripture or not, there was no uncertainty about the pecuniary obligations which his new functions imposed, and that there was, in this respect, a striking coincidence between the privileges of an Episcopal warden and a Presbyterian trustee.

All these changes had happened a dozen years ago, as the stockings in Mrs. Limber's basket could attest, representing as they did—besides Sam, the eldest boy, now a college graduate and student in a metropolitan law-school, and his sister Bessie, the children of the first marriage—

three little Limbers of a later growth, of whom
the eldest was ten and the youngest four, all
boys.

The well-disciplined clocks were about to
strike, in concert, half-past eleven, when Mr. Limber's step was heard at his front-door, and he
was soon seated, with slippered feet, before the
bed of coals which his wife had carefully gathered
into a glowing heap.

"I am out of all patience, Martha," said the
tired warden, "with these vestry-meetings. It
is always the same old story, more debt and less
money."

"How much is wanted to clear off the debt ?"
asked Mrs. Limber, throwing a shovelful of ashes
over the coals.

"Three thousand dollars to cover everything,
including the assessment for opening Shuttle
Street, and the rector's salary to November 1st,"
replied Mr. Limber, with as much precision as
if he were reading the disagreeable figures to the
assembled congregation.

Mrs. Limber deposited another installment of
ashes on the apex of the coal-heap, and flattened
it with the back of the shovel. This was done
with emphasis. She was about to surprise Mr.
Limber with a statement.

"You may count upon Mrs. Chancel and me for a thousand, perhaps fifteen hundred dollars."

"Where from?" inquired Mr. Limber. His monosyllables had a very skeptical tone.

"From a church fair," replied Mrs. Limber, tossing the remnant of the ashes on the extinguished embers, and speaking with as much assurance as if she had announced an entirely original and unprecedented, as well as infallible, remedy for all cases of ecclesiastical poverty.

Her husband shook his head. "A church fair, Martha, is a kind of pious fraud, which can be winked at when its object is to help along a mission-school, or a poor-hospital, or some struggling congregation in a wild parish, but for a congregation like our own, and in a community such as this, it would be too undignified. I had rather put my hand in my pocket and pay the whole debt myself."

And, so far as putting his hand in his pocket went, Mr. Limber suited the action to the word.

"Nonsense, husband!" said Mrs. Limber; "you shall do no such thing. It would be very foolish and very wrong. The people would depend upon you instead of depending on themselves, and, as for dignity, poor and proud may

do for private people, but it will not do for
churches."

"Any thing but a church fair," said Mr. Limber, still unconvinced.

"Except a church debt," rejoined his wife.

"Church debts are bad enough, I admit, but
they are honest debts—certainly ours is—while
a church fair, or any fair, in fact, always seems
to me like a contrivance to get a great deal of
money for very little value, by putting off un-
marketable goods on unwilling purchasers at ex-
orbitant prices, on the pretense of doing good.
False pretenses, I say."

"It is lucky for you, husband," said Mrs. Limber, good-naturedly, "that Mary Chancel isn't
here to hear you charging her and me with false
pretenses. Our fair is to be conducted on the
strictest business principles. We shall have over
six weeks for preparation, and it will be just before Christmas, so that everybody can buy pres-
ents of us; we shall have the best of goods, at
fair prices— "

"Which are always *unfair*," interposed Mr.
Limber—

"I mean moderate prices and you knew that
well enough, so you need not trip me up; but
seriously, David, it will be an advantage to the

whole place. We shall get money, besides, from every one who has it to spend. The Presbyterians are the richest people in Spindle, and why should they have Christmas without paying toll for it to the church?"

"It does seem to me," said Mr. Limber, "that Christmas is the last thing in the world to grudge to any one, even to Presbyterians, if they have the grace to keep it."

"Then let them keep it like Christians," said Mrs. Limber, "instead of locking up their churches and lighting up Christmas-trees which Mrs. Chancel says are relics of heathenism, handed down from the Roman saturnalia, when they lighted wax-tapers in honor of the sun at this very season, and she says that, for all the religion there is in a Christmas-tree, you might as well give the children the Odes of Horace translated into words of one syllable."

"I don't know anything about the Odes of Horace," said Mr. Limber, "nor about Saturn, except that I believe he devoured his children, and it strikes me that Mr. Chancel might as well try to gobble up all the Presbyterian boys and girls as to undertake to cut down their Christmas-trees. But I am half asleep, and the clock is just going to strike twelve."

"I am wide awake," said Mrs. Limber, "but we must try to get down to breakfast earlier on Sunday morning, and going to bed after midnight is hardly the way to do it."

She took up her basket and looked lovingly at the pile of stockings, as she followed her husband.

"After all," she said, "my evening's work was harder than yours:

> 'A man may work from sun to sun,
> But a woman's work is never done.'

Twenty stockings and only one without a hole. Dear me! what shall we do with these children's toes?"

CHAPTER II.

It was one of the sayings of Spindle that the Limbers never did anything by halves. David Limber was a practical manufacturer, with a genius for invention which helped him to reduce the cost and enhance the quality of his fabrics, and fitted him for a competition with rival mill-owners by which he became used to transactions on a large scale, and to very liberal ways. Mrs. Limber, with a constitutional distrust of all retail weights and measures, preferred unbroken packages and uncut pieces. There was thus an air of profusion about their way of doing things which inspired respect. David Limber was justly reckoned by his fellow-townsmen a whole-souled man, and Mrs. Limber was rated as a whole-souled woman—enviable titles, inasmuch as men and women with whole souls were as rare in Spindle as they usually are in other manufacturing or un-manufacturing communities.

It was no wonder, then, that when Mrs. Limber came in her own proper person to the rescue of St. Parvus, and was officially announced in the *Spindle Freebooter* as the promoter and chief patroness of a fair, to be held in her own spacious parlors, and which was to be the most attractive entertainment of the approaching holiday season as well as the most effectual means of relief for a deserving object, it seemed to everybody the most natural thing in the world, and the most certain of success. The beaux and belles of Spindle were on the alert for a new social sensation, and the most satisfactory results of the enterprise were assured in advance, just as an expected financial movement is discounted by the bulls and bears of Wall Street. Volunteers flocked to Mrs. Limber's standard, and her arrangements were soon completed.

"We are making splendid progress," said Mrs. Limber to her husband, as she filled his coffee-cup at the breakfast-table, one Monday morning early in December; "Sam is our treasurer, and Bessie our in-door manager. The stores sell us goods at wholesale prices, and give liberal donations besides. We have a special agent who is making purchases in New York and Albany, and securing consignments of Christmas goods for sale on commission. We are to have a post-office, a Sibyl to tell fortunes, a lovely blonde for an Undine, and half a dozen brunettes for a gypsy camp, a fountain of lemonade with several Rebeccas, a Punch and Judy, a conjurer, a picture-gallery, a pavilion for refreshments, a score of flower-girls, and last but not least a hundred-dollar doll, Mrs. Chancel's special contribution, direct from Paris, with a wardrobe complete."

Mr. Limber had not paid much attention to his wife's list of attractions, but he pricked up his ears at the mention of the last item in the catalogue.

"Who wants a hundred-dollar doll?" he inquired.

"Any one who can get it. The doll is really a work of art. She is to be raffled for at a dollar a chance, one hundred chances."

"Bessie," said Sam, pausing over his tenth buckwheat cake, "I will give you a name for that doll."

"What's in a name?" said Miss Bessie, who was just at the age of the most familiar quotations.

"There is one hundred dollars in the name I am about to propose. If she is to command a hundred, she is a female centurion, and taking a slight liberty with terminations, I christen her 'Centuria,' which you see has this great advantage, besides its evident appropriateness, that, when her expensive wardrobe is to be marked, the initial C. will stand at once for her name and her price."

"What a very smart boy our brother Sam is!" exclaimed Bessie; "I wonder if we couldn't exhibit him as a separate department of the fair, and raffle him off at the end?"

"Not at a dollar a chance," said Sam, returning to his buckwheats.

"Mother," said Mr. Limber, laying down his knife and fork, with great deliberation, and looking seriously at his wife, "do you really mean to have raffling at this fair?"

"Certainly," said Mrs. Limber, in her cheerful, positive tone.

"I am very sorry," said her husband. "I think you ought not to allow it."

"I do not agree with you, husband. I cannot see any harm in a raffle at such a fair as this is to be; they have them at all the church fairs, and they contribute to the enjoyment, and bring in money which we need so much."

She said this so sweetly, and out of the abundance of a heart so full of charity, and a conscience so void of offense, that David Limber was on the point of dropping the subject, without further question or protest, but he found himself impelled by a vague sense of disquiet, rather than by any well-defined motive, to hazard a fresh objection.

"I think, at least I have an impression, that raffling is a wrong thing—morally wrong, I mean."

"Really," said Mrs. Limber, "I don't see and I can't see how a thing can be wrong that is simply and solely to do good, and that too for the church."

"But even for the church," urged Mr. Limber, "ought you to do good in a bad way?"

"How can a way be bad which leads straight to a good end?" rejoined his wife; "the money goes just as directly into the treasury of the church by the raffle as it does by the plate you pass round on Sunday, and every one who gives has value received in the one case as much as in the other."

"I believe," said Mr. Limber, shifting his ground, "that raffling is against the law."

"Oh, I don't know anything about the law," said Mrs. Limber, "and, if it comes to that, a thousand things are against the law, such as woodcock before the Fourth of July, or paying more than seven per cent. or six per cent., which is it,

for borrowed money, and, when I was in New
York last month, Mr. Bullion told me he had been
fined five dollars for having a dead dog carted
from the avenue in front of his house—that was a
violation of the health law, and one of his neighbors had to tear down a new bay-window—that
was a violation of the fire laws; and things have
come to such a pass that it is against the law for
men, in some places, not for women to be sure,
to work more than eight hours a day. Law indeed!" said Mrs. Limber, pressing her evident advantage, " what kind of laws can we expect, when
you send such fellows to Albany to make them
as Jack Filch, a do-nothing and know-nothing,
without an honest hair in his head; and, after one
winter in the Legislature, his wife told Jane Byass, the dressmaker, that she wanted her dresses
to out-trim every lady in Spindle, Mrs. Limber included; those were her identical words—and that
reminds me, Bessie," continued Mrs. Limber in
the same breath, suddenly changing her position,
and giving the subject under discussion literally
a cold shoulder, "that Mrs. Byass has not sent
home that pink silk which you were to have had
without fail last Saturday night. You must go
for it yourself directly after breakfast. Dear me !
what shall we do with these dressmakers ?"

During Mrs. Limber's remarks her husband had wisely resolved to abandon his attack upon the raffle for the present, and to renew it at the dinner-table, trusting to his ability to reënforce his own views by some opinions or arguments to be gained from authoritative sources in the interval. He was therefore well pleased with Mrs. Limber's sudden diversion, and rising from the table he took leave of her in his usual affectionate way, and hurried to his factory and the varied occupations of the day, which embraced a wider range than the circle of his own affairs, for no one in Spindle held so many places of trust as David Limber.

Dinner was wellnigh dispatched when, with what seemed to him a bold plunge, he opened upon Mrs. Limber with the query—

"My dear, have you consulted Mr. Chancel about this raffling project?"

"Dear, no! I should as soon think of consulting him about the pattern of a polonaise."

"It seems to me that the clergyman of a parish ought to be the very best person to decide whether a thing which his parishioners are going to do for the benefit of the church is right or wrong."

"Oh, in the abstract, I dare say—anything, for

instance, that could go into a sermon or about
which there is an article of religion, or a decree
of a council, or something of that sort—but how
perfectly absurd it would be to preach about
raffling ! Besides, dear, good Mr. Chancel is just
as ignorant about practical, every-day matters
and what people ought to do and ought not to
do as ministers always are. You know, husband,
he is as innocent as a babe. Mrs. Chancel says
herself that he is such a piece of perfection that
she has to do things every now and then that are
the least bit wicked just to keep up his belief in
original sin."

"If she can't keep him sound in the faith on
that doctrine," said Sam aside to Bessie, " no-
body can."

"For shame, Sam ! Mrs. Chancel ' is all my
fancy painted her.' She's lovely, she's— "

"When your fancy paints her tongue," said
Sam, " I will let you have my sharpest razor for
a model. It is one of the kind that ' works deceit-
fully ' sometimes."

"Be quiet, Sam, I want to hear what papa is
saying."

"I was talking with Mr. Proser this morning," Mr. Limber went on to say with considerable emphasis, "about raffling ; and he thinks it

should be wholly condemned, on principle. He regards it as very pernicious. He says it is against divine law and human law."

"Mr. Proser is a Presbyterian," said Mrs. Limber, with her usual cheerful terseness when on the defensive.

"For all that, I suppose a Presbyterian can form an opinion and give information on moral subjects."

"Oh, to be sure; as for information, no one can give more than they can. That is what Mrs. Chancel says about Presbyterian clergymen, that they are always imparting information, even in their prayers, where there is certainly the least need of it; and Dr. Flatfoot spends nearly as much time in reading notices as Mr. Chancel does in delivering his sermon."

"Mr. Proser is not a clergyman," said Mr. Limber, "but he is certainly a most upright, excellent man, as everybody knows."

"So he is," said Mrs. Limber heartily, as if it was a joy to her to speak the best she could, even of Presbyterian human kind, "he is just as good as he can be, and as patient as Job with those harum-scarum children of his, but he is not responsible for all Spindle, nor is he infallible, so far as I know. As Mrs. Chancel says, his good

3

ness is of the nitro-glycerine sort—you can't
come in contact with it without its exploding and
blowing you to bits."

"But, my dear, Mr. Proser is a man of great
experience, his views are entitled to respect; he
is an elder in the church, he has been to the General Assembly, and he knows what he speaks
about. He says that raffling is gambling, and a
raffle is a lottery, and he can see no difference or
distinction between the two."

"None so blind as those who won't see,"
said Mrs. Limber; "Mr. Proser will never forgive
me because you chose to leave Dr. Flatfoot
and become a churchman. He can make differ-
ences and distinctions fast enough when he
chooses. He thinks it sinful to take a glass of
wine at a wedding, but you ought to see him de-
vour brandy-peaches and tipsy-cake when he can
get them. He thought it was dreadful to go to
see Ristori in 'Queen Elizabeth,' but he sends
his family in a body to the Hippodrome and
the Minstrels. There's a nice distinction! But,
as Mrs. Chancel says, there are some people who
will make a wry face over a quadrille and gulp
down a circus."

"My dear Martha," said Mr. Limber, "I have
no doubt Mrs. Chancel is a good woman, but I

do wish you would not quote her all the time. With all her sharpness she can't lift her own baby, and I'll be bound she doesn't darn her husband's stockings. If I am wrong about this matter, I will stand corrected, but I don't want to be pelted with Mrs. Chancel's smart speeches. I would rather have a pound of your plain homespun common-sense than a bale of her sarcasms."

Feathered with this touch of flattery, Mr. Limber's shaft, aimed apparently at Mrs. Chancel, found its way to his wife's heart. She laughed good-humoredly as she replied:

"Why, husband, I thought Mrs. Chancel was your particular admiration. She is all the time sending her love to you. As for lifting that little Dicky, I think she might do it now and then if she would make an effort, but I should be quite as well satisfied if she kept his face clean, poor child! And now I think of it, speaking of children, I promised to look up old Widow Riley and those orphan grandchildren of hers. They have positively nothing to eat. I must go there before dark. Do give me some money to leave with them."

Mr. Limber produced his pocket-book and responded to his wife's appeal. He could not

retrace the precise steps by which the result had
been reached, but he was conscious that his pro-
mulgation of Mr. Proser's views on raffling had,
by some succession of ideas, led to a contribution
of five dollars for the benefit of a deserving family and to nothing else. Mrs. Limber, however,
seemed entirely satisfied, and, with the money in
her hand and a kiss on her lips, she parted from
her husband intent for the time being upon her
charitable errand.

"Come and take a look at Centuria," said
Bessie to her brother Sam, when they were alone
in the dining-room, "here she is in the bottom of
the cabinet;" and by the opening of the doors the
waxen beauty was disclosed, in all the plenitude
of her Parisian toilet.

"The true girl of the period," said Sam,
"chatelaine and all; what an assortment she has
dangling there—a fan nearly as large as herself,
an umbrella, a watch, an opera-glass, vinaigrette,
card-case, pencil, reticule, eye-glass!—why don't
you hook on a prayer-book, Bessie? Somebody
may mistake her for a Methodist."

"Not with that point-lace trimming on her
dress," said Bessie; "they say that belonged once
on a time to the Empress Eugénie."

"How did Mrs. Chancel ever come into possession of this supremely ridiculous piece of personal property ? " inquired Sam.

"Some fine lady of her acquaintance picked it up in Paris at a sale, and, hearing about our fair, has sent it to Mrs. Chancel, who makes it her special contribution. That is the story, I believe; 'I tell the tale as 'twas told to me.' But dear Sam, do you know I am half sorry we have the doll on our hands. I have an idea that something disagreeable will happen. Papa seems so opposed to raffling."

"What did Mrs. Chancel say when she heard of his objections?"

"She said that some people's consciences were like her boy Dicky, always waking up and creating a disturbance when they ought to be quietly asleep. I think that was very disrespectful to papa, don't you? and besides, it was hardly kind to say of Dicky."

"Dicky," said Sam, "is not too young, it seems, to point a moral, though he is too ugly to adorn a tale. Mrs. Chancel did not mean to be disrespectful to papa, but she does not intend to be interfered with. The raffle is decreed, and to abandon it now would be like giving up one of the thirty-nine articles."

CHAPTER III.

PAT LOONEY'S LUCK.

MRS. LIMBER's visit of mercy had carried light and love into a dark place. She came home with the reflected glow still lingering on her face, and with thoughts of kindness and sympathy filling her heart. Mr. Limber being occupied with some business visitors, she went earlier than usual to her bedroom. On entering, she was surprised to find Bridget, a housemaid of several years' standing, the most trusted of her servants, engaged in smoothing pillows already as smooth as pillows could be, placing chairs in position, and doing other unnecessary things with evident embarrassment. Mrs. Limber's divination-cap was on in a moment. She scented trouble. Her thoughts flew at once from their tranquil height to the dead level of domestic cares.

"Bless me, Bridget, what is it?"

"Please, ma'am," said the girl, dropping a half courtesy, "I was just waiting-like for you, to give you warning that I'm leaving when my month's up, and it's up next Monday, it is."

"What do you mean, Bridget; has any thing gone wrong down-stairs?"

"Oh, no, ma'am," said Bridget, brightening into confidence in her haste to repel any such idea; "I have no fault to find with any one in the house, leastways yourself, and Mr. Limber is an awful nice gentleman, he is, and the children are all good, and Miss Bessie is a fine young lady, and Mr. Sam—"

"Well, what in the world takes you out of a good place? Perhaps it is nothing, after all."

Bridget grasped the solid foot-board of the bedstead, and looked down on the carpet; at last she mustered courage to say, without looking at her mistress:

"It's Pat Looney, ma'am."

"Pat Looney!" Mrs. Limber gave the name an inflection which operated somewhat after the manner of a patent corkscrew in making an opening for Bridget's pent-up feelings. She looked up, and they flowed freely.

"Yes, ma'am, Pat Looney, you mind, him as was always speaking for me, and it's three years we have kept company, and now he wants to be married next week, and—"

" You marry that shiftless fellow! Bridget,
you ought to be ashamed of yourself—a nice,
tidy, capable girl like you. Why, he hasn't done
a stroke of work this twelvemonth. I have seen
him hanging around the Spindle Shades, the lowest kind of a drinking-place, and I wonder he
hasn't been killed outright in some drunken
brawl! Have you lost your senses, Bridget?"

" Well, ma'am, Pat has been idle at times
like, which it is a weakness in his bones and
pains, and his being there was all along of a light-
ness in his head; and that is gone now, and he
has just come to his luck, ma'am, and he can live
without work if he chooses."

"How can Pat Looney live without work?
If he is an honest man he cannot do it."

" Please, ma'am, maybe Pat wouldn't like me
to be telling it, but it's a lady you are, and you
wouldn't get me into trouble, and it's himself
that has drawn a prize on his policy-ticket, he
has, and he has got the money, he has, and it's in
the bank, it is, and it's three thousand dollars, it
is, ma'am."

" Drawn a prize in the lottery!" cried Mrs.
Limber; " three thousand dollars on a policy-
office ticket, and now you mean to marry him!
Why, Bridget, I never heard of such a thing in

all the days of my life. It is sheer, downright madness. The man will go to destruction, and drag you down with him, as sure as you live, and you will never have a day's peace. Those policy-shops are the vilest places in the world, and drawing a prize in them is worse than losing your money, because a man never does a day's work after he has once drawn a prize; and, like drinking, it goes on from bad to worse! Before I would marry that man, Bridget, if I were you, I would scrub the cross-walk in the middle of Main Street on my bare knees in broad daylight!"

"But, indeed, Pat has done no wrong," said Bridget, whose self-possession was wholly restored by Mrs. Limber's violent onslaught; "sure it was his own money he paid for the policy, and he took his chance with the rest, and if Pat Looney's luck is better than theirs, where's the harm, and him with his mother to help; and it was for a good end like, if it was to help him to marry, for the priest says a good wife is from the Lord, though it's meself that says it, and the end scarifies the means, he says."

"Sanctifies the means, Bridget," said Mrs. Limber, "and that is nothing else than a false Jesuit doctrine; and as for Pat Looney's luck, it is all chance and a wild-goose chase; the next time he will lose everything he has got, and more besides."

"But you see, ma'am, it was all along partly because of Pat's vow, it was."

"What vow could he possibly make about such a wicked thing as a lottery-policy? Vow, indeed!" said Mrs. Limber, in a blaze at Pat's profanity.

"Sure and it was a vow that he would give five dollars to the church out of every hundred dollars, if his ticket was lucky, and he has kept his vow sacred, and it's meself that is just after coming from the priest, and Pat counted the money into his hand, and he gave us his blessing, he did, and a good man is Father Mahoney, and it's good to us both his blessing will do."

"Bridget, this is horrible," said Mrs. Limber, "to go and throw yourself away in this fashion, and then to mix up religion and vows and the church with these dreadful policy-shops! I do think Father Mahoney ought to be ashamed of himself, but it's all of a piece—like people like priest. You marry that man, and you are a ruined girl. Your husband will be a gambler and a drunkard all his days, and perhaps a burglar or a murderer, and he will end in the State-prison or on the gallows. This is just as certain as the sun is to rise; gamblers will stake their money, and their wives, and their children, and their own souls, until every thing is lost. If I had known or suspected that any girl in my house was mixed up with such wickedness, I should have dismissed her on the spot, the moment I found it out. I hope to goodness he has never brought any of his hateful lottery-tickets into this house!"

"And indeed, ma'am," said Bridget, turning on her heel and giving her head a toss, "it's very hard you are on poor Pat for drawing as honest a prize as ever was drawed in a lottery, seeing you are going to have one yourself, by what I hear, to keep your own priest's head above water, which it is himself can't do at all; and it is a true saying, that 'people who live in glass houses shouldn't throw stones at their neighbors.'"

And Bridget sailed ont of the room and down the hall before Mrs. Limber could recover her breath.

"Is the girl crazy?" she said to herself, and then, as the full meaning of her parting words dawned upon her, she added, more amused than indignant, "was there ever such impudence? Our innocent little raffle, for the best of causes, compared to a vulgar lottery! You might as well compare our Sam to Pat Looney."

And, as Mrs. Limber, with a little more vigor and rapidity than usual, loosened her dress and jerked off her undersleeves, she relieved her feelings with the exclamation:

"Dear me! what shall we do with these Biddies?"

CHAPTER IV.

A RUBRICAL RECTOR.

MR. LIMBER, without knowing that his conscience was like Master Dicky Chancel, found it a very restless companion. It kept up a perpetual buzzing, like one of the great fly-wheels of his own factory, and set in motion all manner of doubts and questionings as to the propriety of the raffle, and new reasons why he ought to bestir himself in opposition, in spite of Mrs. Limber's positive off-hand assurances in its support.

"There is no use in arguing or contending with the women when they are bent on having their own way," was his sensible conclusion after a long course of reflection. "I will try Mr. Chancel myself. If I am wrong, perhaps he will set me right; and, if I am right, he must interfere and put a stop to Mrs. Limber's raffle. I ought to have gone to him before."

The little rectory adjoined the church of St. Parvus, and in fact was connected with its rear

by an old woodshed, to which Mr. Chancel, with
the aid of the village carpenter, had striven to
impart the air of a mediæval cloister, but with
indifferent success. The rector's study was on
the ground-floor, and commanded a view of his
front-gate. In this study, somewhat scantily
equipped so far as as his professional needs were
concerned, the most imposing article of furniture
was the worthy rector himself. He was not a tall
man nor a large man, nor was there anything
striking in the expression of his smoothly-shaved
face, his broad forehead, or his rather dull blue
eye. But he was intensely clerical in his ap·
pearance, and carried himself as though he was
perpetually in full view of a congregation. In-
tellectually he was afflicted with a mild confusion of ideas respecting the cure of souls, church
creeds, communions, forms, and furniture, under
the force of which he had gravitated into that
extreme wing of the church militant which, by
its own movements, has most effectually severed
its communications with Christian charity and
common - sense. His small, natural light had
thus been hopelessly hid under a bushel of the
densest ecclesiasticism. Mrs. Chancel herself
was accustomed to say that he had been let down
from the surface of the earth at an early age into

a church school, and then a little deeper into a church college, and then deeper still into a theological seminary, from the lowest depths of which he had tunneled off into a succession of clerical employments on the same dead level; and while wandering in these catacombs she had fallen in with him, and he had married her, which, the lively lady always added, he never would have done had he seen her by daylight.

Aside from the injustice to herself, Mrs. Chancel's description was hardly overdrawn. Her good husband, not content with the quiet duties and rewards of his country cure, fancied himself a theologian and a polemic, and was best satisfied when excavating in some contracted and subterranean vein, which had its local fire-damp, and occasional explosions, but rarely enabled him to make any contribution to the upper world, beyond an occasional fossil or the vertebræ of some extinct animal. And yet, at heart, and when off his rickety stilts as a High-Churchman, Mr. Chancel was a good fellow, fond of a quiet joke, true to his high function, and yet easily remitted to the good things of this life, of which, in truth, he had but a short allowance, and even priding himself on his skill in brewing a kind of patristic punch, which in his earlier days

was in great vogue in certain thirsty corners of
those same catacombs whereof Mrs. Chancel
spoke.

Mr. Limber's appearance at the rectory-gate,
in the forenoon of a week-day, was almost as
great a surprise to Mr. Chancel as if one of the
early fathers, whose devotion to the church he
humbly strove to emulate, had suddenly de-
scended to the sidewalk. His first impulse was
to rush up-stairs and exchange his morning
dressing-gown for the rigid clerical costume, by
which he endeavored in his daily walk to inspire
the people of Spindle with a due reverence for
the cloth. But Mr. Limber had already caught
sight of the rector, and was on the porch. The
magnetism of his genial presence drew Mr. Chancel to the door, which he threw wide open to
give free entrance and welcome to his parishioner.

"My dear sir, this is an unusual, an unexpected pleasure. Walk into my study; will you
seat yourself in this easy-chair? I trust Mrs.
Limber is well, and your lovely family. You
appear to be enjoying your usual excellent
health."

Mr. Limber reciprocated these cordial greet-
ings, and seated himself with more than ordinary

deliberation, feeling quite at a loss how to introduce the topic which had induced his visit.

But the worthy rector was eager to seize the opportunity of interesting his visitor in the line of excavation which he had immediately in hand.

"You find me hard at work, Mr. Limber," said he, waving his hand in deprecation of the disordered state of his study, and his own unpresentable attire, various portions of which indicated that, though Mrs. Chancel's needle might be as sharp as her tongue, it was not as ready for active service; "I am engaged on the sixth sermon in my course on the rubric, which I may mention to you in confidence will be extended to twelve, and which I propose to give to the church, I may say the world, under the title of 'Caput Ecclesiæ, or the Rubric reinstated,' the chief title, as you perceive, being an adaptation, I trust not inapt, of the ancient ecclesiological designation of that part of the church in which the altar, I will not say high altar, was erected according to the canons of Gothic architecture, and the minor, or sub-title, indicating the great need of the church at the present time — the need of what we may call, Mr. Limber, a new rubrication. I trust, sir, you are alive to the im-

4

portance of this great subject. You stand by the rubric, do you not, Mr. Limber?"

"It is rather fine print," said Mr. Limber, evading the question.

"Yes," said the rector, with increasing animation. "Lamentably true. 'Rubric,' Mr. Limber, is an equivalent term for 'Law.' The ancient Romans, as you perhaps remember, entitled their laws with red letters, and yet the modern Church abandons this most essential symbolism, and the rubric is seen in black, a symbol itself of a degeneracy from which I hope to take a humble part in rescuing the Church. The rubric should be in large, conspicuous Gothic characters, and in the original color which belongs to it; you say well, Mr. Limber. I rejoice in the incidental confirmation of my views afforded by your wise suggestion."

"I was not aware," said Mr. Limber; "that you laid so much stress on the rubric. I thought it was your sailing directions, so to speak. I did not suppose it was chart and compass."

"The common error," said the rector; "rubricity, Mr. Limber, is the sheet-anchor of the Church. Take a single but conclusive example, the deplorable abuse of joint communion between churchmen and non-churchmen. The rubric is explicit here and settles the case. It reads, ' And there shall none be admitted to the Holy Communion until such time as he be confirmed or ready and desirous to be confirmed.' Now let us throw it into the form of a syllogism : no one can confirm but the bishop, consequently no one can rightfully commune unless confirmed by the bishop, consequently only confirmed persons can commune together. Here you have the grand principle of church exclusion, Mr. Limber; but let me read you an extract from my sermon on which I am now engaged, in which I undertake to demonstrate that the commandments, although read according to the rubric of our Church at the right side of the altar or ' table' as our Prayer-Book unfortunately has it, and not at the north side, according to the rubric of the mother-Church, are virtually read in the same place, inasmuch as in either case, by tradition and ecclesiastical understanding, the place where the altar stands is theoretically the east, and therefore—"

Mr. Limber's internal fly-wheel was buzzing with immense velocity. He made an effort and broke in abruptly :

" My dear Mr. Chancel, pray let me hear that another time. I ran in, at an odd moment, to speak with you about the church fair which the ladies are getting up. You know about it, I presume."

" Certainly," replied Mr. Chancel, depositing his manuscript on the table with evident reluctance. " I am aware that it is in contemplation and preparation. A most meritorious service. Church fairs are of great antiquity. Like the rubric, they are of Roman origin, as the name indicates—*feria*, a holiday. Servius Tullius, I believe, established a fair at which the laws were proclaimed; afterward they were consecrated by being appointed on saints' days, and you may remember that, by royal grant, the Bishop of Winchester received the revenues of the fair of St. Giles, which lasted for sixteen days, during which all merchants who sold wares in the city or within seven, some say seventeen miles of it, forfeited them to the bishop. A noble tribute to the Church, Mr. Limber."

" Rather an impracticable one in our day," said Mr. Limber, hastening forward several centuries and bringing the conversation directly to the day and date then present; " but about this fair of our ladies, which I suppose is all well enough meant, it seems to me that there is one thing which they intend to do that is wrong, and I have come to ask you about it."

Mr. Chancel looked at his parishioner with a mildly expectant air, strikingly in contrast with David Limber's energetic speech.

"It is the raffling that I mean; setting up a hundred-dollar doll and other nonsensical things, I dare say, to be raffled for. It appears to me that this is against good morals, and I believe that it is against the law. The fair is to be held in my house, and I do not want to violate either morality or law, and I would like to know what you think about it and whether you will use your authority to prevent it."

"I presume, Mr. Limber," said the rector, with great deliberation, "that you address this question to me, not in my individual capacity, but as the incumbent of this parish."

"Upon my word," said our honest manufacturer, feeling the ground beginning to slip away from him here, as it had done at his own table, "I want to know whether this thing is right or whether it is wrong, and I do not see that it makes any difference whether your opinion is given in your dressing-gown or your surplice."

"The point of my inquiry is this," said Mr. Chancel, pursuing the even tenor of his speech, "right and wrong are relative terms, Mr. Limber, and, in the case supposed, the answer might de-

pend upon varying considerations, presenting in
one aspect an abstract proposition, and in the
other a question of expediency. Even lotteries,
under certain conditions, have been comprehend-
ed within the category of pious uses. A temporary structure is said to have been erected at the
west door of St. Paul's on one occasion for the
drawing of prizes in money, plate, tapestry, and
armor; and I believe it is customary, as an ad-
junct of a strictly eleemosynary character, to
make a moderate use of the lot or chance in connection with fairs of this description. Personally, as a speculation in the higher region of
morals, I might discuss the subject with you
casuistically; but, should it be, and I am unable
to affirm the contrary without further information, that the bishop of this diocese, upon due
deliberation, or even by implication, as by his
presence or expressed approbation, had sanc-
tioned the holding of a fair at which such an ac-
cessory was introduced, it would ill become me
to hazard an official decision that this was erro-
neous. I will never commit an act of contumacy
against my bishop, Mr. Limber, never; and I
should hesitate to pronounce a private judgment
where the subject is one which might properly
be referred to my superior for adjudication."

"But, if it is against the law of the land," urged Mr. Limber, "are you not bound to take note of that, and instruct your parishioners?"

"Not in the present absolute, I will not say unhappy, divorce of Church and state," rej lied the rector, promptly. "You will bear me witness that I have never preached politics or meddled with the civil powers. No, sir, I am clear of that imputation, however obnoxious to it other pulpits may be."

"Other pulpits" meant Dr. Flatfoot, who had just preached and published a sermon telling some plain truths about the habits of the manufacturing population of Spindle, giving the statistics of drunkenness and crime, and demanding an enforcement of the Sunday and excise laws. But Mr. Limber was too much occupied with the subject in hand to notice this side-thrust.

"Then I am to understand," said he, rising and turning toward the door, "that it comes to this, Mr. Chancel—you decline to interfere."

"Just so ; to interfere—the precise word, my dear sir. Etymologically, it is derived from the Latin *inter-ferio-ferire*, "to strike between "—a most apt derivative and descriptive word, giving you, as a practical man, my exact position. It is in many instances the duty of a priest to strike against the foes of his church, but never to strike between friends or to foment occasions of discord. A bishop is to be no striker, and certainly a poor rector should not be one."

Mr. Limber shook hands and said good-by as cheerfully as he could, but with a feeling that somehow he was being baffled at every point, and as if it were his own fault. There was an awkward sense of discomfiture in his leave-taking, but Mr. Chancel's was as genial as at his first greeting.

"Good-by, my dear sir—my best regards to Mrs. Limber. You will be sure to come again; my next sermon will interest you as a manufacturer. It will be on the symbolism of vestments, and, by-the-way, I may mention to you in confidence that, in that discourse, while I establish the identity of the surplice with the *isiaca* of the priests of Isis, I utterly confute the absurd Puritanical prejudice against it on that account. Come again, Mr. Limber. I rely upon you as a rubricist."

If the front-gate closed with something of a slam it in nowise disturbed the serenity of the good rector, who went back to his excavations with a complacent smile, after lighting a pipe, which looked as if it had been bought at the first fair after the discovery of tobacco.

CHAPTER V.

MR. LIMBER walked from the rectory at a rapid pace, in the direction of his factory, with the full intention of reaching that haven of rest at the earliest possible moment. But, as he turned the corner of the street which led from the Broadway of Spindle to the manufacturing district, he suddenly stopped. Mr. Limber was an inventor, and, like other inventors, he had his sudden inspirations. He hesitated for a moment, as if to assure himself that he was right in obeying the new impulse which controlled his movements, and then deliberately turned about and retraced his steps toward the main street, saying as he did so, " Why didn't I think of John Calendar before ? "

John Calendar was the best of the half-score of lawyers who went up to the circuits and general terms of the judicial department in which Spindle was situated. Being a man of method and moderation, with a horror of debt, and a habit of paying his bills promptly, he had acquired a reputation for wealth, and, being a man who was more given to thinking than to talking, he had also acquired a reputation for wisdom. In reality he was neither as rich nor as wise as people supposed, but, as he made no pretensions to either quality, it was not his fault if he was doubly overrated. On the other hand, he was even a better lawyer than his clients imagined, and, besides his knowledge of the law, he was versed in many things, among others in human nature and the ways of the world.

Mr. Calendar was a stanch Presbyterian, and yet it was he who had counseled David Limber, when he sought his advice, to quit the First Presbyterian Church, and go with his wife to St. Parvus. "Do not hesitate," he had said to his client and old friend, as he saw him wavering under a conflict of views, "go with your wife, by all means; you will change neither your religion nor your creed; the family is older than the church. You are only a private and not an officer in the Presbyterian ranks, and are not responsible for the system, nor is it with you a matter of sentiment as it is with your wife; to her the church-life to which she is accustomed is a part of her being, and she never could be at ease elsewhere, while you can accommodate yourself easily to a change. For personal piety the church of Jeremy Taylor and Wilberforce ought to be as good as the church of Calvin or John Knox. Its form of government would be intolerable to me, but it will not disturb you. Its order of worship is superior to ours—"

"I didn't suppose you would admit that," said Mr. Limber, somewhat startled.

"Certainly I do, not to the praise of Episcopacy, but to the blame of Presbyterianism. The Anglican Church, or its American offshoot, has no more exclusive right to the Te Deum, or the prayers of the early fathers, which they have taken from the Latin Church, than they have to the Lord's prayer or the Apostles' creed, but as a squatter's title is sometimes made good by prescription, our Presbyterian churches, following a bad extreme of Puritanism, leave them in possession of the liturgy. It will be a great comfort to you, at least it would be to me, to be in a church where you will have some idea beforehand what is going to happen at a christening, a wedding, or a funeral. I would be an Episcopalian myself if it were not for Episcopacy."

"The service is very monotonous," said David

Limber, feeling bound to make some show of resistance.

"Yes," said Mr. Calendar, "it certainly is, but it is the monotone of the deepest needs and highest aspirations of our fallen, redeemed humanity, and, to the English-speaking race, the book of Common Prayer must ever be, next to the Psalms of David, the most perfect medium of intercourse between earth and heaven which the spirit of devotion ever cast in the mould of human speech."

Aided by such counsel as this, Mr. Limber, to whose honest nature substance was more than form, was easily won over to the Prayer-Book, submitting for its sake, as he used sometimes to say, to a great deal of sing-song in the sermons. This happy result was mainly due to Mr. Calendar's good offices, but Mrs. Limber never knew for how much of her domestic peace and happiness she was indebted to the sharp-eyed lawyer, whom she was apt to regard as a bigot in his religion, an ascetic in his life, and a bore in his conversation.

Mr. Limber was fortunate enough to find the lawyer in his office, a little building adjoining the old-fashioned house which he had made thoroughly comfortable according to his own ideas, after the somewhat luxurious though not extravagant habits of his profession. He greeted his client very cordially.

"I thought I should have a visit from you this week. We shall begin to take testimony in the patent case next month, and I want the list of your witnesses."

"It was not that which brought me here to-day," said Mr. Limber, seating himself by the table and going at once to his point. "I want to ask you some questions about another matter. Perhaps I am foolish about it, but you must settle it for me. You have heard of Mrs. Limber's church fair that is to be."

"Yes, to be sure. Our Lillie is working for it like a little beaver."

"Well, Calendar, they are bent on having a raffle at this fair which I suppose is a common thing, but I have got it into my head that it ought not to be, and I want to ask you first of all this simple question: Is raffling right or wrong?"

"Unquestionably, wrong."

"Do you mean morally wrong or wrong because it is against the law?"

"Both. It is wrong by itself and in itself, and wrong, besides, because the law of the land prohibits it."

" Very good, but now I want you to tell me
why it is wrong and how it is wrong. I want
you to explain this thing and lay down the law
to me, both as to the moral part and the legal
part, just as if I were a jury and you were a
judge or a chief-justice."

And Mr. Limber put on a concentrated air of
attention, befitting twelve single jurors rolled into
one, waiting for the judge's charge at the close
of a long trial.

" The moral part, as you call it," said the
newly-invested chief-justice, " is very simple. It
rests on two plain facts which no one can dispute.
Fact number one, that there is in our human nature,
no matter how it got there, an inherent, universal disposition to make chance a means of gain ;
fact number two, that this natural passion serves
no good end, and, on the contrary, has always
and everywhere, the world over, proved a fruitful
and perpetual source of idleness, misery, and
crime, so much so that the most advanced communities absolutely prohibit its exercise, either on
a large scale in government lotteries, or on a small
scale in bar-room raffles or church-fair raffles. In
other words, society says to every man, woman,
and child, that to pay money or give any valuable
thing for the chance of gaining a larger sum or

something of greater value, is so pernicious a thing in itself and in its effects that it shall not be tolerated. This is the testimony of society to the moral evil, and here comes in what you call the legal part; because the evil is so universal and far reaching, our own State has undertaken to stamp it out by the most solemn prohibitions."

"I was certain it was against the law," said David Limber, eagerly.

"Against the law! My dear sir, the prohibition is made a part of the constitution of New York. This is a very different thing, you see, from a law, which one Legislature may make and the next Legislature repeal."

"That disposes of my wife's Jack Filch argument," said Mr. Limber to himself.

"Yes," continued Mr. Calendar, "this prohibition is a part of our social compact; of the fundamental law, as we lawyers call it. Let me read it to you."

"That is right," said Mr. Limber. "I like to have chapter and verse."

"Very well, here it is, article first, section tenth of the constitution, the last clause: '*Nor shall any lottery hereafter be authorized or any sale of lottery tickets allowed within this State.*'"

"But does that include raffles?"

"Yes, it does; the word 'raffle' is only another name for 'lottery,' the difference being that, in a lottery, money is paid for the chance of winning money, and in a raffle, money is paid for the chance of winning some article of more or less value. The word 'lottery' in the constitution covered both descriptions, and when the Legislature came to make laws, to enforce the prohibition of the constitution, it used both words, 'lottery and 'raffle.' I will read the law to you presently, but, just now, let us keep in mind that the provisions of the constitution and the law rest on the conceded moral mischief of the thing. What is condemned is not made wrong by the law, but the law condemns it because it is wrong. So you see that a lottery or a raffle is an immoral and illegal thing, not to be permitted on any pretense whatever, whether to put money into the exchequer of a State, the purse of a gambler, or the treasury of a church. Have I made this clear to you?"

"Perfectly," said David Limber, "but I must ask one or two more questions: has it ever been decided by the courts that a raffle is wrong and illegal if it is in aid of a good object? That is my wife's strong point. She says that a raffle like hers, for a purely good object, cannot possi-

bly be against good morals or against the law.
Has such a case ever come up?"

"Certainly it has, and before our highest
court. I will tell you how it came about: There
was hardly ever a more commendable object in
itself than the American Art Union. It was an
association devoted to the promotion of the fine
arts and the encouragement of American artists.
Any one could subscribe, and by paying five dollars, yearly, become a member. The money was
used to maintain a free gallery for the exhibition
of works of American artists, to issue to each
member a fine engraving every year, and a copy
of the *Art Journal*, published monthly by the
association, and to the purchase of original paint-
ings by American artists. Thus the subscriber
received for his five dollars, in the use of the gallery, in the engraving and the journal, and in the
satisfaction he took in the promotion of American
art, a full equivalent for his money, and he was
interested besides, as a part owner, in all the
works of art purchased during the year by the
association. At the close of the year, all the
pictures were distributed by lot among the mem-
bers, and each one had a chance of getting a
picture worth perhaps fifty, perhaps five hundred
dollars, a landscape by Durand, a classic head by

5

Gray, or a mountain-dell by Kensett. No wonder the Art Union was popular; its fine gallery
on Broadway was a centre of attraction and a
new incentive to the pencil of every artist. In
1851 no less than thirteen thousand subscribers
were enrolled, yielding the handsome sum of six-
ty-five thousand dollars for the cultivation of
American art. All of a sudden the statute pro-
hibiting raffling was set in motion against this
praiseworthy association and its philanthropic
managers, including one very learned judge, several very learned lawyers, and a number of very
eminent citizens, all of whom were arraigned as
violators of the law."

"What became of the case?" asked Mr.
Limber, as much interested as if he had been the
holder of an Art Union certificate of membership.

"It went to the Court of Appeals. The Art
Union made a brave fight. The ablest counsel
pleaded for it; the good it was doing and the
pure motives of its promoters were fully conceded
by the court, but there stood the law and the
constitution, and the fact that the scheme was
wrought out by an appeal to the universal passion
of playing at games of chance brought it under
the ban. As you like to have chapter and verse,
I will take the book which contains the decision,

and read you the very words, so that you may be sure I am not speaking after my own notions, but according to the settled law. Here is what the court say: 'The prohibition was not aimed at the object for which lotteries had been authorized, but at the particular mode of accomplishing the object. It was founded on the moral principle that evil should not be done, that good might follow, and upon the more cogent, practical reason that the evil consequent on this pernicious kind of gambling greatly overbalanced in the aggregate any good likely to result from it.' "

"But, suppose," said Mr. Limber, "the money contributed to the raffle goes to the good object directly, as to the church in this fair, the chance of winning the prize being merely the instrument or vehicle of an act of benevolence, does that make no difference?"

"No, not the least, so long as the chance is the inducement held out to attract the contribution. Whoever holds it out sets in motion the evil principle which is the root of gambling and its legion train of vices. To be sure, with many persons it may be a matter of indifference whether they win or lose, and charity may be the ruling motive. But, in reasoning about the matter, we must take human nature as it is, and men and

women as they are, and the chance of winning
appeals to a universal passion. Suppose two
men sit down to play 'seven-up,' each with fifty
dollars in his pocket, and they agree to stake all
their money on the game, but whoever wins shall
give it all to an orphan asylum. Would these
two be any the less gamblers because the result
of their game was to benefit the orphan? If
charity was their motive, they could each give
fifty dollars without the play; and if amusement
was their object, they could play without the
stake. The real zest of the game is in the hazard."

"Do you mean to say, then, that all games of
chance are wrong?"

"By no means. Chance is a proper element
of calculation and determination, and using it for
amusement is no more wrong than using it in
drawing a jury, classifying directors, or distribut-
ing seats in the House of Representatives; but
to stake money on a chance, whether a cent or
a fortune, whether for greed or benevolence, is
wrong, because it is the exercise of a natural
passion whose tendency is wholly evil, and which,
therefore, must be evil in itself."

"But if it is a natural passion is it possible to
prevent its exercise?"

"No," said Mr. Calendar, "it is not possible. The native love of gaming is like the sea, with its mighty under-currents and its resistless tidal forces. All that human law-makers can do is to build breakwaters which may restrain it within some visible bounds, but which do not stay the incessant roll of the waves or hinder the wrecks which strew the shores. But surely all good men and women should join hands to drive the pest of pious gambling from the church; there, if nowhere else, things evil in themselves ought to be wholly prohibited."

"I think I see your distinction," said Mr. Limber. "It is the stake that makes the moral mischief. According to this, I suppose, card-playing for amusement is innocent, and yet I have never seen a card in your house. This is rather aside from our discussion, but I wish you would tell me why you exclude cards if you don't think it wrong to play cards."

Mr. Calendar smiled as he replied: "My dear friend, you and I might certainly sit down of an evening and take a hand at whist with Mr. Chancel or Dr. Flatfoot, just as Archdeacon Paley was fond of doing with his clerical or lay companions, without breaking any law, human or divine, and we ought to brook no man's meddling

with our right to do so.   I know that St. Chrys-
ostom denounced play as an invention of the
devil, but I believe, with Jeremy Taylor, that so
long as the play is not for money, cards are as
innocent as push-pin, and, if necessary to assert
my right to such an opinion, I would play cards
on my front-porch.   We should never permit
priest or presbyter to recast the moral law or
override the gospel precepts with human prohibitions.   In things not evil in themselves and ser-
viceable for health, or amusement, or social relax-
ation, the Bible rule, as I read it, is temperance
and not abstinence.   And yet, if I am satisfied
by experience and observation that cards are such
favorite instruments of vice, all the world over,
so easily available for the worst uses and so asso-
ciated with every scene of vile companionship,
that I prefer not to admit them to my house, and
to choose other forms of amusement for myself
and my children, I have certainly the right to do
it, though I have no right to impose my pref-
erence on others.   In short, I believe in the
law of temperance and the liberty of abstinence.
But see, and there is this plain difference between
card-playing and raffling, and this may bring us
back to our subject, that one may play at cards,
so long as he does it for amusement only and in

play-time, without infringing any law of morals ; but raffling is wrong in itself, because it stirs up the evil element within us, the love of gaining by chance. It is not a question of the object of the action, but of the character of the action, and, if that is bad, the action must be bad."

"And yet, while the moral evil must of course have always been the same, how is it that the legal prohibitions are so recent? Haven't I heard that Union College, and other literary institutions in this State, were founded or aided by means of lotteries, and the newspapers every day advertise drawings in other States ?"

"Oh, yes! The American Revolution, a more beneficent enterprise even than Union College, was promoted by a lottery, devised most ingeniously by the same immortal Congress of 1776, which put forth the Declaration of Independence, and, to-day, distressed commonwealths at home and abroad resort to the same shifts. In New York we have grown rich enough and moral enough to shame the venerated signers of '76 or our own legislators of sixty years ago, who jumbled together Union College, Hamilton College, the College of Physicians and Surgeons, the Asbury African Church, and the Historical Society, in one grand conglomerated scheme for a lottery

'for the promotion of literature, and for other purposes!' And yet, even now, the spirit of '76 is
not extinct, and, in practice, our people are quite
ready to ignore the constitution, as well as the
moral law, and public opinion winks at the
offenders."

"What seems strangest to me," said David
Limber, "is that I cannot get my wife, who is,
as I verily believe, the best woman alive, to admit the bare idea that her raffle may be wrong."

"My dear Limber, that is simply because
raffling belongs to a class of misdeeds, the evil
of which must be perceived by induction, and
not by intuition. The pure moral instinct, which
would be shocked at the staking a dollar on the
green cloth of the faro-table, takes no wound
when the same dollar goes into the lily-white
hand of a Sunday-school teacher, to swell her list
of raffle-chances. In reality, the same bad passion is appealed to in either case, for different
ends, but, to make this apparent, requires a process of reasoning, and no lady patroness of a
Charity Fair will endure to have her way blocked
by a syllogism. Pure women, with their wits
about them, are wonderful detectives of vice, however masked, but, under the sway of feeling,
they have been arrant law-breakers from Mother
Eve down."

There was a pause, which Mr. Calendar occupied in sharpening a lead-pencil to a very fine point, while his client's brows were contracted under the seeming pressure of some inventive idea. At last his face lighted up.

"You said you would read me the law. I suppose there is some penalty or punishment for breaking it."

"I meant to have given you chapter and verse of the law, just as I did of the constitution. Here it is on page 665 of the first volume of the Revised Statutes."

"Let me hear it," said Mr. Limber, as eagerly intent as if the promised extract were the most entertaining bit of prose ever penned, instead of the two dry sections of the statute which are the hinges whereon our story turns.

Mr. Calendar, thus urged, read as follows:

"'SECTION 22. No person shall set up or propose any money, goods, chattels or things in action, to be raffled for, or to be distributed by lot or chance, to any person who shall have paid, or contracted to pay, any valuable consideration for the chance of obtaining such money, goods, or things in action. Any person offending against this provision, shall forfeit three times the sum of money, or value of the articles so set up, together with the sum of ten dollars, to be recovered by and in the name of the overseers of the poor of the town where the offense is committed.

"'SECTION 23. No person shall raffle for any sum of money, goods, or things in action, or become interested in the distribution of any money, goods or things in action, by lot or chance. Whoever offends against this provision shall forfeit ten dollars, to be recovered as directed in the preceding section.'"

"Thank you," said Mr. Limber, now wholly at ease, and with an air of conscious mastery. "If I understand it right, the threefold value of the thing set up, and the ten-dollar penalty against everybody who takes a chance, are collected by the overseers of the poor."

"So says the statute."

"And who sets the overseers in motion?"

"Any one who will turn informer and make a complaint; but I am quite sure no one in Spindle will think of setting the dogs of the law on these benevolent ladies, even if they are wrong-doers."

"Can the overseers refuse to act if they are called on to enforce the law?"

"Strictly speaking, I suppose not. The law presumes that every public officer is as prompt to do his duty as he is to draw his pay."

"And the overseers can sue every man and woman and child who has taken a chance?"

" Yes, for ten dollars each."

" And they can sue the person putting up the raffle for three times the value of the thing to be raffled for, and ten dollars besides ? "

" Such is the law."

" Now, Calendar," said Mr. Limber, rising, " one thing more. I want you to make me a bill for all this advice, and date it to-day and receipt it, for I mean to pay it before I go, and I am going now."

Mr. Limber was evidently in earnest, and the lawyer, seeing this, checked the refusal which was rising to his lips, and laughingly said:

" For the legal part of my advice you may pay, but not for the moral part. When my advice is given from the Revised Statutes or from my law-books, or from my own experience or brains, my clients ought to pay, but I can hardly make the Bible a basis for a fee."

" Perhaps you are not quite as sure of your position on the Bible as you are on the Revised Statutes, else why charge for your law and not for your morals ? "

" Perhaps, friend Limber, it is because I prefer to give my clients gratuitously what I think they need the most ! "

" Then you don't always believe in charity

beginning at home ? " said the manufacturer, un-
strapping his pocket-book.

" Take out an X," said Mr. Calendar, while
he wrote and dated a receipt, according to Mr.
Limber's request. That gentleman examined it
carefully, placed it in his pocket-book, and, with
a warm hand-shake, took his leave.

Mr. Calendar resumed his seat at his desk. His
pencil, although he had not written a word with
it since its last sharpening, seemed to require renewed attention. He devoted himself for some
time to the process of giving it the finest im-
aginable point, with an abstracted energy, which
might have served for the cross-examination of
the most unwilling witness. All the while he
was thinking rapidly. At last he pocketed the
pencil, seized a sheet of note-paper, and, taking
up the pen which had just traced Mr. Limber's
receipt, he wrote as follows :

SPINDLE, *December* 10, 18—.
Overseers of the Poor of the Town of Spindle.

GENTLEMEN : I believe that you rely upon me to attend to any law business which you may have. I am
so situated at present that I may not be able to act
for you, and should you require any professional services, allow me to recommend, as a competent and
faithful attorney, Mr. Richard Folio, of this village.
He studied law with me, and was admitted at the last

General Term. He is a prompt and efficient practititioner. Yours truly,

JOHN CALENDAR.

Mr. Calendar, having sealed this note, directed it to "Hugh Boulder, Esq., overseer of the poor," and then opened his window and beckoned to his man-of-all-work who was engaged in repairing a piece of fence hard by.

"Jacob," said he, "did you see Mr. Limber as he left my office?"

"Yes, sir," said the man, touching his hat; "he stopped and asked me whether Mr. Boulder had got into his new office yet, over the bank, and I told him he had. I saw him moving in yesterday."

"Very well," said Mr. Calender; "I want you to take this note to Mr. Boulder's office and if it should reach there as soon as Mr. Limber, or before, so much the better. Give it to his clerk and let him deliver it."

"All right, sir," said Jacob, who was used to Mr. Calendar's explicit orders, which he prided himself on executing to the letter, and he hurried off on his errand.

The lawyer crossed the snow-covered bit of lawn between his office and his house. Midway he was met by a fair-haired, blue-eyed girl of seventeen..

"Dear papa, I was coming to find you. I want you to take a little sleigh-ride with me ; the pony is at the gate."

"Bring me some extra wraps and I will venture with you, and, stop a minute, Lillie"—as the girl turned to fly toward the house—"here is something to spend at Mrs. Limber's fair."

He handed her the ten-dollar note for which he had just receipted to Mr. Limber.

"Oh, thank you, papa, ever so much"—this with a kiss between every two words—"I can buy lots of things for Christmas."

"But, Lillie, not a cent for the raffle."

"No, papa, I should not have thought of taking a chance in it, even if you had not spoken about it."

"And why not, Lillie ? do you think you could make out that it is wrong."

"Really, papa, I had not thought anything about the right or wrong of it. I knew very well that you disapproved of it, and that was enough for me."

And with another kiss she left his side and ran toward the house.

Her father followed her with a look of satisfied affection. "After all," he thought, "love is the fulfillment of the law."

CHAPTER VI.

THE FAIR.

THE fair was a success. This was the popular verdict at an early hour in the day. A light snow-fall, on a well-packed surface, had made the sleighing excellent, and it was all the more enjoyable because of its novelty. The mercury stood just below the freezing-point, and yet the sun was shining as brightly as if its sole purpose was to contribute all its attractive forces in aid of Mrs. Limber and St. Parvus.

Spindle took kindly to a holiday in advance of Christmas, and the well-filled tables in the large, square parlors of the Limber mansion, with their pretty-faced and prettily-attired attendants, did not lack for customers. Everything went on well and everybody was pleased. There were no dead-letters in the post-office; the Sibyls gave out the most flattering oracles and responses at the rate of twenty-five cents each; the gypsies foretold the most auspicious destinies; the fair Rebeccas dispensed unceasing draughts of lemonade from wells in which there was only too much water; Punch and Judy out-Punched and out-Judied themselves in tenderness and tragedy; the conjurer exhibited a cabbage-head in any gentleman's hat; the picture-gallery, wisely ignoring high art, brought the broadest grins to the faces of the visitors; the flower-girls got the largest prices for the smallest bouquets; the refreshment-tent, inclosed in a temporary wooden structure, adjoining the dining-room, and heated with portable stoves, grew warmer as the day advanced, but was always chilly enough to provoke unlimited demands for hot viands and repeated cups of coffee; while the decorations of evergreens and flowers and flags, and emblazoned texts and inscriptions inciting to a reckless benevolence, conspired to produce what the worthy rector was pleased to call a happy and symbolical blending of nature, patriotism, and piety.

Conspicuous on a marble pier-table, in front of a polished mirror, stood Centuria, in all her wondrous finery, and from her satin-slippered feet depended the list of subscribers, duly numbered from 1 to 100. The chances, at a dollar apiece, were taken quite freely, but to fill the roll a little active canvassing was required on the part of the young ladies in charge of the raffle, which was under the general superintendence of Miss Bessie Limber. Every new-comer, especially if he belonged to the not very numerous class of eligible young gentlemen who somewhat sparingly adorned society in Spindle, was attacked with an avidity which would have been creditable to a veteran life-insurance agent. Dialogues such as this were frequent:

"Now, Mr. Diagonal, I declare you must take a chance in the raffle."

"Thanks, Miss Tarleton, I believe not."

"Oh, but you must; we shall never fill it up if you don't."

"Wait till I come this way again."

"How provoking you are! that is just an excuse to get away. I shall lose you if you go."

"I shall lose my money if I stay."

"But you will be sure to get this lovely doll, and you know it will be just the thing for your little niece—what a darling she is!"

"Oh, I never have any luck."

"You never had me to pick you out a lucky number. Now, Mr. Diagonal, I will never, never speak to you again as long as you live and breathe, if you don't;" and, under the influence of this

6

fearful threat, down would go Diagonal's name
and his dollar, the helpless victim receiving in return a sweet smile and a card containing his number.

The evening brought the gentlemen in full
force, and the ladies in fresh costumes. Nothing
so brilliant had been seen in Spindle for many a
day. Mrs. Limber had worked with a will, and
had levied her contributions upon all available
sources of supply. Still, in her heart of hearts,
she wished the fair well over, and the feeling that
she would never—no, never—undertake another,
was beginning gently to steal over her even in
the hour of her triumph. She had planned a visit
to New York before the holidays, and it was arranged that the whole family should leave for the
city the day following the fair. The preparations
for their departure, and the arrangements for putting the house in order during their absence, had
given Mrs. Limber an added share of labor, and
she rejoiced as the evening drew toward its close.
There was to be an auction at ten o'clock, then
the raffle, and all was to end as near eleven as
possible.

This programme had been agreed to in the
morning, and an additional motive for rigidly adhering to it was the presence of the Spindle

brass band, which had volunteered to play at intervals during the evening, and it was only too well known that this tuneful brotherhood had brass enough and wind enough to play all night ·on the slightest encouragement.

Prompted by Mrs. Limber, Sam announced, precisely at ten o'clock, that an auction-sale of all the unsold goods would forthwith be held, immediately after which the drawing of the raffle would commence, the whole number of shares having been subscribed and the books closed. Upon this, one of those good-humored, good-looking gentlemen, who always happen to be present on such occasions, gifted with a ready flow of wit and a magnetic voice, mounted the library-steps, and, after the most approved manner of the auction-room, invited the freest competition, premising that, as he had been waiting all the evening for just such an opportunity of saying his best things, the sale would be, on his part, wholly without reserve.

With such a brilliant auctioneer the sale went on swimmingly. He made more than the usual complement of stale jokes, he dwelt fondly on some articles and knocked down others before they were fairly set up, and bid in several lots for himself, to inspire confidence in his statements of value, and rejected ten-cent bids with scorn, and finally, under the pressure of circumstances, accepted an advance of five cents, and called upon sundry old bachelors to invest in infants' wardrobes, and recommended smoking-caps to gentlemen who never smoked, and shaving-soaps to gentlemen who never shaved, and wound up by offering, to the highest bidder, Mr. Limber's house and furniture, including all the family portraits, with immediate possession ; terms, cash, payable to the auctioneer. In the gaslight and under the evergreens and in the current of good spirits, all this seemed very funny, and the good-humored and good-looking auctioneer had to stop now and then and take breath and wipe his forehead. At last, having cleared the tables, he paused and inquired if there was anything or anybody else he could knock down.

Here some one suggested that everything was sold, including most of the purchasers.

Then some one else proposed that the list of subscribers to the raffle be offered for sale, deliverable after the drawing.

"All right," said Sam Limber, who, as treasurer, was interested in swelling the receipts by every possible penny, " set it up and sell it on that condition."

"Here it goes, then," said the auctioneer, "this unique and valuable list of subscribers, the only one in existence, every name warranted to have been written by the subscriber in person or by his duly-authorized attorney and therefore invaluable to an autograph-collector: what shall I have for it?"

"Five dollars," promptly responded a voice in the corner of the room.

"Five dollars is bid, less than one-half its value—will you say six—then five, seventy-five—five, fifty—five, twenty-five—five, fifteen—five, ten—five, five—are you all done?—going, going, last call, fair warning—gone, at five dollars, to—whom shall I say?"

"Richard Folio," was called out from the corner.

"What does all this mean?" said Mrs. Limber, who, supposing that the auction was ended, had been giving her attention to something else for the moment.

"It is Dick Folio," said Mrs. Chancel, who was at her elbow; "he has had the list of subscribers to the raffle set up at auction and has bid it off for five dollars."

"He hasn't five dollars to his name," said Mrs. Limber. "He was Mr. Calendar's office-boy or clerk, and I don't believe he has made a cent since he set up for himself."

"Perhaps it is his way of advertising. He gets his name before the very best people in Spindle, in connection with the respectable sum of five dollars, attracts attention, makes a sensation, and gets himself discussed."

"I should hardly think any one would stop to discuss Dick Folio."

"But, my dear, we are discussing him."

"Well," said Mrs. Limber, "he will never pay the five dollars."

"But he is paying it now."

And, sure enough, Mr. Folio was, at this very moment, handing to Sam, in full view of the two ladies, a veritable five-dollar bill of the unimpeachable issue of the First National Bank of Spindle.

"Did you ever!" exclaimed Mrs. Limber. She could not tell why, but she felt a shiver of uneasiness, as she saw the transaction closed, to the evident satisfaction of the purchaser.

There was no time for further remark on this episode, as the drawing of the raffle was about to begin.

To insure absolute fairness in this important proceeding, two highly-respectable gentlemen carefully examined the counters, on which were inscribed the numbers, from 1 to 100, and then deposited them in the bottom of a tall, china vase, after duly inspecting it to ascertain that it was entirely empty. The counters were then well shaken up by the same impartial hands. A very young lady, in white muslin, with bare arms, was then blindfolded, and, after having been turned round several times, to her utter confusion, was led to the vase, into which she was directed to plunge her arm five successive times, and each time to bring up from its depths a single counter, the fifth to be the winning number. This fivefold trial of fortune was in order to prolong the excitement of the drawing, and to give the additional zest of showing how tantalizing, as well as capricious, the blind and fickle goddess may be.

The little bare arm went deftly down into the vase, and brought up the first counter. The brace of respectable gentlemen examined it, and one of them called out the number, and then the good-humored and good-looking auctioneer with the magnetic voice read from the list the name of the owner. This happened to be one of the belles of Spindle, who thereupon received a round of condoling applause. The second name was that of an elderly maiden lady, who gave a little scream when her name was called, which set everybody laughing, to her great displeasure, as the one thing she never could put up with, under any circumstances, was to be laughed at. There was no time for explanation or apology, as the next name was waited for with an impatience which increased as the drawing progressed. The third name was that of a young gentleman who declared that his chance was guaranteed by the young lady who took his money, so that he didn't care whether he won or lost. The fourth was none other than the good-humored and good-looking auctioneer himself. This made a hubbub of laughter and applause, during which he pretended to faint, and was brought to by the aid of the parlor-bellows.

This performance was very exciting, and even Mr. Limber, who was watching it from a remote corner, caught something of the infection and felt a genuine thrill of expectancy as the little bare arm went down for the fifth time, and, in the profound silence, drew from the vase the lucky number. The two respectable gentlemen examined it, and then one of them read it aloud, "*Sixty-three.*" The good-humored and good-looking auctioneer glanced at the list and looked up with a puzzled air. The pause heightened the suspense. He seemed for the first time a trifle disconcerted, but the writing was plain and so was his duty, and the magnetic voice read "*Number Sixty-three—Bridget Looney!*"

There was dead silence, then a titter and a sudden disappearance of a little group of housemaids, who had slyly gathered at the door leading from the butler's pantry into the dining-room— and then a general murmer, as if something had gone wrong and a universal grievance had been distributed among the guests. The idea that this name, so wholly unknown to fame and to the select circles of Spindle, was the *alias* of some lucky subscriber, who had sailed into success under false colors, was freely suggested, while the imputation that Mrs. Limber would permit any one but her guests to compete in the raffle was indignantly rejected. And yet it was a mystery which no one volunteered to solve. Evidently the good-looking auctioneer, with all his humor, had no joke in reserve for such an emergency as this, and he looked a little foolish. Mrs. Limber's quick eye had turned at once on Bessie, whose face wore the deep crimson of detected guilt. Sam caught a glimpse of the truth and, with rare presence of mind, signaled the band, which immediately struck up "Home, Sweet Home," a loud hint for leave-taking.

"For once," thought Sam, "a brass band is a blessing."

Mrs. Limber, whose forebodings were only too clearly defined, drew Bessie into the bay-window of the library.

"What is the meaning of this? How in the world did that odious Bridget's name get on the list? We are all disgraced!"

"Dear mamma, it is my fault, but I really could not help it. I will tell you how it was. Bridget came to me the night she left us. I did not know until then that she was to be married, and she reminded me that I had promised her, ever so long ago, and I had, that whenever she was married I would give her a wedding present. 'Now, Miss Bessie,' said she, 'it is only a little trifling thing I want you to do for me; your pa and ma have been good to me, and yourself, and it's no present I'm asking.' I told her, without thinking, that I would do anything I could for her, and she kept saying, 'Oh, it's easy enough,' and so I pretty much promised her, just as we do sometimes, you know, with the children when they tease. 'But what is it, Bridget?' I asked her over and over. Then, when she had got the

promise, she said: 'It is just nothing at all but
a chance in your ma's lottery.' Of course, then,
I told her she must not call it a lottery, and I
tried to put her off, and proposed that I would
take an extra share in the raffle, and pay for it,
and if I drew the prize it should be hers; but,
'Oh, no, miss, that wouldn't do at all,' it must
be her own money that pays, and her own name
and number, or it wouldn't be 'no good.' Then
I said, 'Nonsense, Bridget, why waste your money just when you want it?' 'Never you fret
about my money, Miss Bessie,' said she, 'but if
you will break your word to a poor girl, and you
a fine lady, it's easier breaking than keeping.'
—Now, mamma, what could I do? What I did
was this: 'Bridget,' said I, 'you are a silly goose,
but pick out your number.' 'The number is
picked already,' said she; 'it's Pat's lucky number, and a happy wife it will be making me, and
it's number 63, it is.' I knew there was only
one chance in a hundred of her winning, so I
kept it to myself, and said nothing to you or to
any one else."

"But I did not see her name on the list. I
looked over it only fifteen minutes before the
drawing."

"No. I just wrote 'taken,' opposite the num-

ber, and, a few minutes before they put the counters in the vase, I wrote the name, 'Bridget
Looney,' in the list. I never supposed that any
one would see it or hear of it, and I don't know
now what she meant by its being Pat's lucky
number and making her a happy wife. She just
threw the dollar in my lap and kissed my cheek,
and ran off. Dear mamma, are we all ruined?
I wish I had never heard of the fair, nor the
raffle."

Hysterics were imminent. Mrs. Limber was
frightened into comparative self-possession, and
she said as quietly and as assuringly as she could:

"Never mind, Bessie, it is my fault for not
telling you what I knew, and putting you on your
guard. Bridget has married a bad man, a gambler who deals in lottery-tickets and everything
that is wicked, and I told her plainly she was
ruined and lost if she married him, and this is
her revenge and his."

"They would have had no revenge, mamma,
if number 63 had not drawn the doll."

"But number 63 has drawn it," said Mrs.
Limber. "No matter, darling; here comes Mrs.
Chancel, and we must not wince even if we are
hurt. She knew Bridget, but she never heard
of her by her husband's name, and does not mis-

trust that it is she who has drawn the French doll. Run and take a breath of fresh air and drink a glass of water, but not too cold, for your blood is all in your face."

"Pray, my dear Mrs. Limber," said Mrs. Chancel, in her biting little way, "how long have you known the Looneys, and who is the fortunate Miss Bridget who walks off with Centuria, as Sam calls her?"

"She seems to be a person who has paid her money," said Mrs. Limber, determined not to be drawn into any explanations, and putting the best face she could on the catastrophe.

"Oh! it's a genuine she, then? I thought that perhaps it might be some *incognita* who had turned Biddy for to-night and stooped to conquer. Is she a princess of Fenia?"

"Perhaps she is," said Mrs. Limber, evidently disconcerted and without an arrow in her quiver.

"You look so very, very tired," said Mrs. Chancel, compassionately, "we ought all of us to go; and Mr. Chancel is waiting in the cold for me. He was having a good laugh over what he was sure must have been a fictitious or symbolical ' Bridget, but I must go and stop it. What a pity! a spoiled joke is so very disagreeable."

Fortunately, the leave-takings of other and

less satirical guests interposed to cut Mrs. Chancel short, and their congratulations and good wishes went far toward restoring Mrs. Limber's equanimity. The necessity of giving her final directions for the night and of seeing that some order was brought out of the chaos of the fair, was a more effectual restorative, and she strove to dismiss, for the present at least, the disagreeable result of the raffle.

"Sam, my dear boy," said she, "take the doll and put it with all its belongings in one of those large paper boxes and leave it on the top shelf of my cedar closet; lock the door and bring me the key. I shall be in my dressing-room. Everything else here is to be placed in the refreshment-room and disposed of to-morrow. I have sent Bessie to bed, and your father went up-stairs half an hour ago."

"I wonder what possessed Dick Folio to buy that subscription-list?" said Sam, as he set about obeying his mother's instructions. "Dick is pretty sharp, and five-dollar bills do not grow on every bush, at least not in a young lawyer's shrubbery."

When Sam brought the key to his mother, she was closing the blinds of her window, according to her custom, and pausing as she did so for a glance into the cold, dark night. Sam looked out with her upon the quiet village.

"What is that bright light in the tall window down there?" asked his mother. "It is after half-past twelve, and everybody who has not had a fair in the house ought to be sound asleep."

"That," said Sam, after a moment's observation, "is the printing-office of the *Spindle Freebooter*. They are doing night-work; very likely setting up some libel against an honest man who is in bed and asleep. Slander is the chief resource of the press, nowadays."

"That is very true," said Mrs. Limber, acquiescing easily in Sam's off-hand, midnight depreciation of the greatest of the powers that be; and she added with a sigh, as she closed the blinds and fastened her window, "Dear me! what shall we do with these newspapers?"

CHAPTER VII.

THE DAY AFTER THE FAIR.

IN spite of the fatigues and excitements of the fair, the Limber family assembled in full force at the breakfast-table the next morning. Mrs. Limber and Bessie were unusually quiet, and their appetites were evidently below the ordinary standard. Sam was in unabated spirits, and Mr. Limber, according to his wont, serenely cheerful.

The door-bell rang.

"That," said Mrs. Limber, "is the man from Delf's. He was to come early this morning to take away the extra china."

The man from Delf's proved to be a boy from somewhere else.

"He is in the hall," said the waiting-maid, " and wants to see Mr. Limber very particular."

"Let him come in here," said Mr. Limber.

" And see that he wipes his feet on the outside door-mat, and leaves his cap in the hall," said Mrs. Limber. " But why not let him wait, husband ?—you never know what kind of places these boys come out of."

But the boy was already at the dining-room door. It was plain enough that the place he had come out of was a lawyer's office. He had in his hands a big bundle of papers, unmistakably legal, tied with red tape, and arranged with evident precision ; and he was equipped with a memorandum-book and a pencil. He was a chunky boy, rubicund of hair and face, somewhat belligerent in his general aspect, and looked as though he might have been, as perhaps he was, the lineal descendant of several generations of deputy-sheriffs. A view of his side-pocket disclosed the fact that he had been engaged in eating a large apple, upon which he had temporarily staid proceedings in order to attend to the business in hand.

" David Limber, Martha Limber, Samuel Limber, Bessie Limber," said the boy, as if he were calling the roll of the entire family, " I have got summonses and complaints for all of you," and he evidently knew by sight the respective persons whose names he had pronounced, for he proceeded, in the most deliberate manner, to draw certain papers from his bundle and to deliver one

7

to Mr. Limber and another to Sam, who was seated at his father's left hand. He then crossed, as formally as though he were following a stage direction, to Mr. Limber's right, and, after a deliberate survey of Bessie, thrust a third paper at her, which he put into her hand without any cooperation on her part, very much as packages of prize-candy and other light wares are devolved on unwilling recipients in railway-cars.

"I would like to know," said the aggressive boy, as the paper fell on Bessie's lap, "whether you are a minor, under the age of fourteen years?"

"What an impudent boy!" said Bessie, turning to her mother.

"Oh, very well; if you decline to answer, I will make sure, and serve a copy on your father, mother, or guardian. I've got plenty of them."

"Oh, I am over fourteen — seventeen last March," cried Bessie, fearing lest she had involved the family in some new trouble by not telling the whole truth instantly, and yet entirely unable to comprehend the behavior of her strange interlocutor.

Mrs. Limber had made up her mind at an early stage of this proceeding that it was in some way connected with the taking of the census, and had

rather enjoyed Bessie's evident alarm ; but there
was something in the tone and manner of this
domineering boy which inspired her with a vague
dread, as he left Bessie after making a careful
note in his memorandum-book, and invaded the
side of the table sacred to the breakfast-tray and
the coffee-urn, and thrust a fourth paper in the
direction of her own proper person. In her repeated experiences of census-takers, she had always found them, though of an inquiring turn of
mind, very affable in their manners and disposed
to deal gently with the subjects of their in-
quisition so long as they were liberally plied
with family statistics.   But this disagreeable
youth had a malevolent look which roused all her
antipathies and apprehensions; she pushed back
her chair, and, spreading out her napkin, as if to
guard against the danger of personal contact,
gave him what she was in the habit of describing
as "one of her looks."   All of no avail ; the un-
terrified boy would have served process on Medu-
sa herself.   Mrs. Limber receded an inch farther.
"How dare you intrude into a gentleman's house
and behave in this indecent way?   I will have
none of your papers," said she, in her most for-
bidding tone ; "you must leave the room and the
house instantly.—Jane, run to the stable and call

Thomas.—Mr. Limber, I am amazed that you allow such impudence to go on ; this boy ought to be punished."

" I've delivered a copy of the summons and complaint to you personally and left it with you," said the boy, deliberately, as he jerked the paper on Mrs. Limber's napkin ; "and you are known to me to be the person named therein as the defendant, Martha Limber, and that's good service whether you choose to take hold of the paper or not; that's all, you needn't call Thomas, he isn't a defendant. Good-morning," and the boy departed, taking an enormous bite of the apple as he left.

Mrs. Limber sat in silence, with her chair still pushed back from the table, the rejected document at her feet, whither the law of gravitation, to which even the processes of justices' courts are subject, had taken it, under the impulse of a little shake of the napkin on which it had lodged. So near an approach to a personal insult she had never experienced as at the hands of this shameless boy, and she was speechless under the shock.

" I declare," said Sam, who all this time had been busily engaged in reading the document handed to him, and also the one which had been served on his father—" I declare this is the coolest thing yet! There never was anything like it in this world."

"Sam," said Bessie, "what is it? Is it anything dreadful?"

"Dreadful? I guess you will think so! It is all about the raffle."

"Then, don't tell me anything more—the very thought of that raffle is perfectly awful. But I suppose I must. Do go on, Sam, tell me all, tell me the very worst—oh, why do you keep me in this fearful suspense?"

"It is a suit at law," said Sam; "the overseers of the poor of the town of Spindle have sued papa and mamma in Justice Hazey's court for three hundred and ten dollars. Just hear this, will you—it is all printed: it says that the defendants—that's papa and mamma—'did, heretofore, on the fifteenth day of December in this present year'—that's short for yesterday, you see—'at the village of Spindle, in the town of Spindle, set up and propose a certain chattel, to wit'—oh, do listen to this!—'an image or effigy of the female, human form, composed, as to the head and neck thereof, of wax, and as to the rest, residue, and remainder thereof, of muslin stuffed with bran, sawdust, or other minute particles'—there's a legal description of a doll for you—'to

be raffled for to certain persons who then and
there respectively paid, or contracted to pay, the
sum of one dollar for the chance of obtaining the
same, there being in all one hundred chances, and
the value of the said chattel so set up being then
and there one hundred dollars '—that's a whop-
per," said Sam—"'contrary to the provisions of
the Revised Statutes of this State; wherefore, the
said plaintiffs '—that's the overseers of the poor,"
added Sam—"'demand judgment against the said
defendants '—that's papa and mamma, you know
—'for the sum of three hundred dollars, being
three times the value of the article so set up '—
I should think it was—'together with the further
sum of ten dollars, making in all three hundred
and ten dollars and the costs of this action '—holloa !   Richard Folio, plaintiff's attorney.'"

"So, Dick Folio is at the bottom of all this,"
said Mrs. Limber.   How utterly contemptible!—
Of course, husband, you will take no notice of
it."

"But dear mamma," interposed Bessie, "why
did he make Sam and me take these horrid papers?"

"Wait a minute," said Sam; "that's only
one suit.   Now here is another against me, and
if your paper is like mine Bessie, I guess there is

another against you. Let me read : 'The overseers of the poor complain of the defendant '—
that's me this time—'and show that heretofore '
—just the same as in papa's—'he raffled for a certain chattel, to wit '—and then it goes on and de-
scribes Centuria, just the same, bran, sawdust,
and all—'wherefore they demand judgment for
ten dollars and costs—Richard Folio, plaintiff's
attorney.' Now, Bess, yours is identically the
same, and they are after you for ten dollars."

"But I have not got ten dollars," said Bessie.
"I spent all my allowance at the fair."

"Then you will have to go to jail," said Sam,
remorselessly.

"Sister Bessie sha'n't go to jail," shrieked
little David Limber, aged six, suddenly aroused
from his oatmeal-porridge to a sense of the calamity impending over the family, and giving a
sympathetic howl, and exhibiting incipient symptoms of strangulation. His mother rushed to his
rescue, and jerking his arms suddenly over his
head—a process by which she had saved many
infantile lives, and repeatedly entitled herself to
the medal of the Humane Society—averted the
catastrophe. Sam was duly reproved for his
heartless remark, and after a penitent disclaimer
on his part and a positive assertion that Bessie

should not go to jail, David was consoled and resumed his porridge, while his elder brother pur-
sued his researches into the papers.

"This thing is all printed," said Sam, "ex-
cepting the names, and they are written in; my
name is written in mine, and your name in yours.
I do believe they have gone and sued every one
of the whole hundred subscribers—just think of
that!"

"That is why Dick Folio wanted the subscription-list," said Bessie, with a sudden access
of light. "It was to get the names to write in
these frightful summonses, or whatever they are
called."

"No wonder he was willing to bid five dollars for it," said Sam; "why, he has got a hundred
suits for ten dollars apiece, besides this big one
against papa and mamma for three hundred and
ten dollars, that makes a hundred and one suits
in one day.—And now, mamma," said Sam, still
pushing his discoveries, "don't you recollect we
saw the *Freebooter* office lighted up last night,
and wondered what they were doing there? It
is plain as day, now, that they were busy printing off these very papers, and Dick Folio had
only to write the names in from the list. Just
think of that boy going all over Spindle this

morning, eating apples and serving everybody with these papers! It was mighty smart in Dick Folio, though."

Mrs. Limber was in a white heat. The truth had slowly dawned upon her. "David," said she, "do you really imagine that all the people who took shares in the raffle are sued for ten dollars a piece by this impertinent Dick Folio?"

"So it would seem, my dear," said Mr. Limber, who was quietly plodding through his breakfast.

"It is too disgraceful to think of," said Mrs. Limber. "You must put a stop to it immediately. Is there no way of having him arrested? And that boy too?"

"Really," said Mr. Limber, "it looks more like his having us arrested."

"And to think," continued Mrs. Limber, "that this same Richard Folio was once a boy in my Sunday-school class, when he was no bigger than our Davy. Of course, he can never, never cross the threshold of this house again."

"It is thirteen hundred and ten dollars, all told," said Sam, still absorbed in the legal documents on which he was making marginal notes and calculations; "and costs besides in one hundred and one suits. Now costs are something that you can't calculate. There is no telling what they may run up to."

"Thirteen hundred and ten dollars," said Bessie, despairingly, "is more than the whole profits of the fair."

"There is one consolation," said Sam; "I paid over all the cash, last night, to Mr. Mix, the treasurer, and they cannot stop that: it was twelve hundred and sixteen dollars and one cent. I have got his receipt for it."

"What on earth have the overseers of the poor got to do with all this?" demanded Mrs. Limber; "do they oversee everybody, and do you suppose that Dick Folio has any right to bring them into his impudent schemes?"

"I believe," said Mr. Limber, "by the law any one who sets up a thing at a raffle is liable to pay a penalty to the overseers of the poor of three times its value and ten dollars besides, just as Sam has read from the paper, and everybody who takes a chance in the raffle is liable to pay a penalty of ten dollars."

"What an infamous law!" said Mrs. Limber, "and then to start it up and set it agoing, between night and morning, against respectable people like us, while thieves, and drunkards, and murderers, and burglars, go scot-free! Who in

the world would ever suspect that there were
any such penalties kept concealed like traps to
be sprung upon honest people in their own
houses, and at the breakfast-table, and by boys
too ?"

"My dear," said Mr. Limber, "every one is
supposed to know the law, and I told you long
ago that I believed the raffle was against the law,
and I warned you to take care, but you went on,
and now it appears that the law is going to be
enforced against us. Respectable people are just
as good defendants as thieves or drunkards, and
at all events those who dance must pay the
piper. That's good law."

"But, papa," interposed Bessie, "why should
they sue you, as well as mamma and us? We
had the raffle, and not you. I thought married
women had everything separate nowadays. I
mean property, and debts, and all that."

"Yes, Bessie, but a husband still has the
privilege of paying for his wife's wrongful acts
when they are done in his presence. I learned
that when I was on the jury, last winter. If a
married lady should, of her own sweet will, but
in presence of her husband, bite off the nose of
another lady, the law would presume that the
biting was his act, and not his wife's, and he, and

not she, would have to pay the market value of the lost nose. That's what they call the common law, I believe."

"It seems very uncommon to me," said Bessie, "but I suppose I don't know anything about it; but, dear papa, another thing," and here she brightened suddenly, "how can they sue me? I am only an infant, Sam keeps telling me, and he says I am incapable of making a contract."

"So you are," said Sam, "but I never said you were incapable of committing a tort."

"What in the world is a tort?"

"A tort," said Sam, solemnly, "is any naughtiness for which you can be made to pay damages. If you were to hire Jack Rumble's pony and phaeton, to go from here to Shuttleville, he could not sue you for the price, because you are an infant; but if you over-drove the pony, as you probably would, and killed him, that would be a tort, and he could sue you and make you pay damages, just the same as if you were as old as Methusaleh."

"But, Sam," persisted his sister, "if I am an infant, how can I know the law? and, besides, infancy ought to excuse a great deal of tortiness or whatever you call it."

"Oh, we have a legal maxim that disposes of any such plea—'*malitia supplet ætatim*.'"

"And what does that mean?"

"It means that, in the eye of the law, the younger you are the worse you are—so there's no help for you, Bessie; you must pawn your furs and pay up."

"Our trip to New York may as well be given up," said Mrs. Limber, in a coldly-despairing tone; "we are doubly disgraced. Last night's experience was bad enough, but this is a hundred times worse. We shall be the talk of the whole town."

"The trip to New York must not be given up," said Mr. Limber, cheeringly. "We will go as we have arranged, and better there than here. I will put this affair in Mr. Calendar's hands, and it will keep till we come back.—Sam, when is the summons returnable?"

"Monday week, eight days; this is a justice's court, you see, and the time is short. But we shall be home on Saturday night, and, if old Calendar doesn't get up some defense, it will be the first time he has failed to do it. Who knows but the law is unconstitutional?"

Mr. Limber shook his head. "There is one comfort," said Mrs. Limber, after her husband had gathered up the papers and taken his departure. "Bridget Looney will have to pay ten dollars as well as the rest."

"She can well afford it," said Bessie; "she gets the doll."

"I did not think of that," said her mother.

"And besides," said Sam, "she has gone off to parts unknown and can't be served."

"I did not think of that either," said Mrs. Limber.

CHAPTER VIII.

THERE was hardly a house in Spindle in which there was not a defendant. If Mr. Richard Folio's object was to make a sensation, he certainly had succeeded, and, if it is an advantage to be discussed, he was enjoying it to the fullest extent. Public opinion, with its usual disdain of fact and law, made up its own case. Dick Folio was denounced as a designing scamp of an attorney, whose innocent victims (a rather ignoble army of martyrs) were walking about Spindle, to the number of nearly fivescore, each suffering under the same summons and complaint, and without an available remedy or defense.

Even those who had taken no chances in the raffle, and who had not been at the fair, were indignant that so many people should be sued. A hundred actions in a forenoon seemed as great an outrage on the community as a corner in grain or an over-issue of stock. Nothing but a criminal

design on the peace of society could have involved a whole population in such a sudden and
unparalleled vortex of litigation. Some of the
more aggressive defendants talked loudly about
blackmail, and hinted that, if the grand-jury were
in session, a case of conspiracy might be made
out and the tables turned on the prosecutors.

With such voices in the air and on the street-
corners, Mr. Folio's personal safety would have
been imperilled, had he been within reach. But
it happened that he had left Spindle, on a business errand, early the same morning on which
he woke up and found himself infamous. After
satisfying himself that the raffle-suits were all
properly launched, he had gone about his other
business, which had been delayed a day for the
express purpose of enabling him to attend to
this exigent prosecution. Rumors of his sudden
unpopularity reached him on his way to the station, in the gray of the dawn, but he had time
only to send a hurried line in pencil, by the vigi-
lant boy, to his clients, the overseers of the poor,
committing his injured reputation to their keeping, before the whistle of the express-train
warned him to purchase his ticket and begin his
journey.

Mr. Folio's office was on a prominent part of

the main street of Spindle, on the ground-floor, and the door was reached by a single step. During his absence the indefatigable boy kept watch and ward over all his interests and posses-sions. Under Mr. Folio's training he had become well versed in the arts, offensive and defensive, belonging to his important though subordinate sphere, and had been specially instructed as to his personal behavior and well drilled in a sort of manual adapted to every emergency of an office-boy who, in his intercourse with chance visitors, might be entertaining clients unawares.

Toward the close of the afternoon this vigi-lant custodian, tired of watching the leisurely snow-storm which was in progress, and having completed a course of light gymnastics, to the detriment of Mr. Folio's office furniture, was quietly engaged in a corner of the room, polishing his shoes. He varied the monotony of this occu-pation by eating an apple and conducted the two pursuits, wholly at his ease, discovering no in-compatibility between them, except the slight flavor of blacking occasionally imparted to the fruit.

While thus engaged he was suddenly inter-rupted by an octavo volume, bound in law calf, which described a curve from the table in the

8

centre of the room to the side of his head, striking it a glancing blow which, without seriously
disturbing his equilibrium, roused him to the con-
sciousness that a visitor required his attention.

"Holloa!" shouted the boy, not speaking
from the manual, "what do you mean by heaving
Blackstone at me, like that?"

"I wish it was a paving-stone," said the
caller, a stout gentleman in a crimson cravat,
with a mottled complexion, whom the observant
boy immediately recognized as Mr. Bender, a
gentleman of sporting proclivities and a perma-
nent boarder at the Spread-Eagle Hotel, who
kept three horses and a dog at Rumble's livery-
stable. "Where's your boss?"

"Gone to Albany, to the Court of Appeals,"
said Mr. Folio's representative, this time according to the letter of the manual. "If there's any
word to leave please write it down, and if it's
money I'll receipt for it."

"I called in to punch his head, that's all,"
said Mr. Bender, turning toward the door.

"If you'll fix a time I'll put it in his diary,
and he'll call and save you the trouble of coming
again," said the faithful youth, still adhering to
the text of the manual.

Mr. Bender looked at him with a vengeful

eye. " I say, you must be the young rascal," he bawled out, " who got me out of bed yesterday morning on false pretenses and poked papers at me through the crack of the door, making believe it was a telegram."

"I guess I am," said the boy, keeping the table between himself and the self-disclosed defendant, with his hand on the inkstand as an available projectile in case of need. " You was the only one out of the whole lot I wasn't sure of, because you look such a heap different when you ain't fixed up. I didn't know but I had waked up your great grandfather and served him by mistake, but you have admitted service and now I'm all right."

Mr. Bender had not been unobservant of the advantage which the inkstand gave to the interesting and ingenuous lad, and contented himself with casting a withering look upon him, and saying in a lofty tone with a few familiar maledictions, that both he and his master had better keep out of his way, especially if he happened to have a horsewhip in his hand; and so, keeping his eye warily on the inkstand, Mr. Bender backed out of the door.

He had proceeded along the street about a dozen yards, when he became suddenly conscious

that a well-packed snowball had flattened itself
on the nape of his neck, at the summit of the ver-
tebral column, and was taking a downward course
along the same manly portion of his frame. He
executed a rapid right-about face, to the infinite
amusement of a crowd of schoolboys, who were
disporting on the sidewalk in the new-fallen snow,
and whom he immediately denounced as the per-
petrators of this gross personal outrage. They
shouted a chorus of denial, and were unanimous
in attributing it, by significant gestures, to an
elderly gentleman with an umbrella and a carpet-
bag, who was making his way along the slippery
pavement near Mr. Folio's office with great difficulty. Mr. Bender instantly and profanely rejected this glacial theory. After a moment of
hesitation and with a spasmodic effort, only par-
tially successful, to rid himself of so much of the
snowball as remained accessible on the top of
his collar, he retraced his steps in the direction
of Mr. Folio's office, to find, on reaching it, the
door securely locked, and the legend conspicuous on the outside—" Gone to supper."

The next morning public opinion faced about,
as rapidly as Mr. Bender had done. The Spindle
Freebooter made its weekly appearance on that
day, and in a conspicuous column appeared the
following :

"CARD TO THE PUBLIC.—The overseers of the poor of the town of Spindle think it proper, in the absence of their attorney, Mr. Richard Folio, to state that the suits brought by them against the parties concerned in the recent raffle were not, in any manner, directly or indirectly, instigated or set on foot by that gentleman. On the contrary, Mr. Folio had no knowledge of the subject until he was employed as the attorney of the overseers, who are solely responsible for the prosecution of the suits, and who intend to enforce the law.

HUGH BOULDER,
Overseer, for Self and Associates."

Mr. Boulder was a well-known contractor who had built most of the roads radiating from Spindle Court-House, and bridged all the streams in the town. He stood over six feet in his stockings, and reckoned his weight by the stone instead of the pound. At convivial gatherings he was accustomed to break pokers over his arm, and at primary meetings he was relied upon to preserve harmony by putting refractory delegates out of the most convenient window. A card from such a source carried conviction. Besides its intrinsic weight, it was aided by a brief editorial comment at the foot. The editor of the *Freebooter* had put his paper to press with a flaming editorial, reflecting public sentiment in the convex mirror of

journalism, with the flagrant heading, "BLUE
LAW IN SPINDLE.—Have we a Blackmailer among
us ?" But Mr. Boulder's opportune appearance,
with his official card, accompanied by an advertisement for certain proposals for building, signed
by the overseers, immediately metamorphosed the
Freebooter into an organ for the prosecution.
The projected editorial was suppressed, and the
press stopped to replace it with the overseers'
card and the following paragraph double lead-
ed :

"The above official announcement will effectually annihilate any disparaging and unfounded
rumors reflecting upon our esteemed fellow-citi-
zen, Mr. Richard Folio, who is universally re-
spected as one of the brightest luminaries of the
Spindle bar. It also sheds new lustre on our distinguished overseers of the poor. Spindle is a
law-abiding community. While, as a manufacturing centre, we claim that the primary object of
all law is the protection of home industry, we
concede that incidental protection to the public
morals is properly within its province. Let the
avenging bolts fall where they may, the *Freebooter* stands immovably on the ancient maxim,
' *Fiat justitia, ruat cœlum !* ' "

A copy of the *Freebooter* found its way, with

Mr. Limber's letters, to his hotel in New York. It contained, in addition to the important matter we have already extracted from its columns, an elaborate description of the fair, in a style more worthy of the genius and gallantry of the metropolitan press than of a rural sheet, and discreetly free from any allusion to the raffle. The compliments showered on the lady managers were profuse, and Mrs. Limber perused the article with a sense of relief and satisfaction. But the card of the overseers failed to convince her of Dick Folio's innocence. She tersely remarked in reference to it that " you couldn't believe anything you saw in a newspaper." This, it is true, was immediately after she had indorsed the article touching the fair as thoroughly accurate, but this slight inconsistency gave her no trouble. If anybody else was imposed upon, she was not, and if she was certain of anything it was that the hundred-headed hydra of litigation which was devastating Spindle had been warmed into life by the cupidity and malevolence of greedy Dick Folio.

Bessie, who was bent on having "a good time" in New York, even if, on her return home, she was to go straight from the station to the Spindle jail, read the account of the fair with sparkling eyes, and fully accepted Mr. Folio's vindication at the hands of the overseers.

"I never thought for a moment Dick would do anything mean," she said; "but, dear Sam, what does *fiat justitia, ruat* something, mean?"

"It means," said Sam, "that, when the sky falls, the lawyers will catch all the larks."

There was still another and less conspicuous paragraph in the *Freebooter* which escaped the notice of Mrs. Limber and the young people, but which, later in the day, and when alone in his parlor, Mr. Limber read with a quiet satisfaction. It ran thus:

"We call attention to the advertisement, in another column, of the overseers of the poor, for proposals for building a hospital-wing. It is to be erected at once, and we have the very best authority for saying that the expense is already provided for without calling upon the tax-payers. At this Christmas season, such an announcement is specially timely and gratifying."

As Mr. Limber cut this editorial notice from the newspaper, and then looked up the advertisement to which it referred, and cut that also from another page, and folded both away in his pocket-book, he seemed well pleased. His inventive expression pervaded his face, and gave it a bright and satisfied air.

"So far, so good," was his brief soliloquy, and he went to his dinner with a complacent smile and a good appetite.

CHAPTER IX.

FIAT JUSTITIA.

JUSTICE HAZEY'S court-room had never before been so thronged as on the return-day of the "raffle-suits," as they had come to be popularly designated. The first resentments had subsided; misery loves company, and the great majority of the defendants were reconciled to a calamity in which there was so large and respectable a companionship. It was generally understood that Mr. Calendar would represent Mr. Limber, the chief victim of the prosecution, and, as he was sued for the considerable sum of three hundred dollars, it was expected that all the resources of the law would be availed of in his behalf. He was known to be a good fighter, and to have succeeded in all his patent-suits. Every defense interposed by Mr. Limber would, of course, inure to the benefit of the other defendants, of whom there were ninety-and-nine, process having been served on every one of the subscrib-

ers to the raffle, with the single exception of
Bridget Looney, who was enjoying her honey-
moon beyond the jurisdiction of the Spindle justice. There was a natural desire on the part of
the ninety-and-nine that Mr. Limber's should be
made a test-case, to be carried through all the
courts of the State, at his individual expense and
risk, and, if possible, to the Supreme Court of
the United States at Washington, a distant and
dimly-comprehended tribunal which disappointed
suitors in State courts are very apt to imagine
would redress all their wrongs, could it once get
cognizance of them on appeal.

Besides the parties immediately concerned,
a large body of spectators had gathered in the
court-room — village loungers and do-nothings,
old vagabonds who came to court every day, in
winter to keep warm at the expense of the town
—a crowd of young people, anxious to see how
their impleaded acquaintances would figure as
violators of the law—and a respectable number
of elderly gentlemen, who sustained the action
of the overseers in the interest of a strict morality. In addition to these, the legal profession
was represented by every one in and around
Spindle who had any connection with the practice of the law, a collection of worthies for whom

nothing could be more attractive than the novelty of a hundred suits, and the prospect of a hundred trials.

Mr. Limber and Mr. Calendar were among the earliest comers. Mr. Folio, with his papers in good order, was seated at the table in front of the justice's desk. Behind him waited the indispensable and now historic boy, furtively enjoying a large pippin, and eying the numerous defendants grouped about him, with the keen satisfaction of a sportsman who has bagged his game.

Sam and Bessie were ensconced in a distant corner, trying to look perfectly innocent and unconcerned. Their mother, whose return to Spindle had revived her earlier sense of mortification, had begged Bessie to remain at home with her, feeling that a stigma rested on the fair name of Limber, which the proceedings in court might deepen into an ineffaceable brand. But Bessie's curiosity was stronger than her mother's fears, and Mrs. Limber finally yielded, parting with her, as Bessie said, as if she were on her way to the block.

The justice had never before been overwhelmed with so large a docket or such an array of parties. He had begun life as a blacksmith, and in his experience at the forge, having never known a horse brought to be shod which did not require shoeing, he assumed, on the bench, that no plaintiff came into court who was not entitled to relief. Accordingly, he administered the law by the universal application of the single, simple principle that judgment must be given in favor of every plaintiff and against every defendant. This rule was ordinarily most easy of enforcement, but now he was sorely puzzled. Here was but one set of plaintiffs and a hundred defendants; his term of office was about to expire, and he was a candidate for reëlection. He took his seat, quite willing that there should be a postponement, and half inclined to exercise the right which the law gave him, of adjourning the case for eight days, without reference to the wishes of the parties. Nevertheless, being a somewhat pugnacious justice, he showed no signs of alarm, and looked as learned as Lord Mansfield, while he called the first case, " The Overseers of the Poor of the Town of Spindle against David Limber and wife."

No adjournment was asked for. Both sides were apparently ready, and the perplexity of the justice was momentarily increasing, when Mr. Calendar rose, with his most forensic air, and pronounced the opening formula of " May—it—

please—the—court," with as much suavity and
gravity as if he had been addressing the Court
of Appeals. There was something in his tone
and manner which inspired half the defendants
with the hope that the overseers and Dick Folio
were to be demolished at a single blow. A dim
foreboding crossed the mind of the aggressive
boy, and he lingered on his apple with a vague
sense of terror. Mr. Calendar seemed to enjoy
the sensation he was making, and dwelt upon
his words. At last he proceeded :

" It appears, your honor, that the plaintiffs,
the overseers of the poor, besides serving the
summons in this case, which was all the law required, have furnished the defendants with a copy
of the complaint. This they were not obliged
to do, but I presume there is no objection to it,
and it fully apprizes us of the claim of the overseers, so that we could answer at once, if it were
necessary to answer at all. But I think there
is a fatal defect in the proceedings, and that,
owing to this defect, neither my clients nor any one
of these numerous defendants is properly in court."

" Dear Sam," whispered Bessie to her brother,
" how can Mr. Calendar tell such a fib ? We are
defendants, and we are in court, and so are all
the others."

"He means, Bess, that we are not in court in the eye of the law."

"The law must be dreadfully near-sighted," said Bessie, very much puzzled, "not to be able to see its own court-room full of defendants ; but perhaps I know now why Justice is always painted blindfold."

"The statute," said Mr. Calendar, after a pause, and measuring his words with even more solemnity than at the outset of his remarks, "requires that the summons shall be served by a constable, but provides that the justice may, when he deems it expedient, upon the request of a party, by a written authority endorsed on the summons, empower any proper person, being of lawful age, and not a party in interest, to make the service. Now, I see, by looking at the summons, that your honor did, at the plaintiff's request, depute a person who is not a constable to serve it, and I am informed that this person is not of lawful age, but is in fact a—"—here Mr. Calendar paused again to give due emphasis to his final word—"a boy ! "

"How do I know that, Squire Calendar ?" said the justice; "the summons is here, and the return is on to it, and it shows good service on its face."

"I believe the boy is in court," said Mr. Calendar, "and I might say that he shows bad service on his face, for it is a very juvenile one; but, if the fact must be proved, as I suppose it must be, we will prove it. There can be no difficulty in showing who served the paper."

"I will swear to the boy!" called out a stentorian voice, in the outer edge of the crowd, near the door of the court-room.

"Silence!" shouted the justice; "this isn't town-meeting."

"Sam," whispered Bessie, "what horrid man is that who called out to the judge?"

"It is Mr. Bender," said Sam, "and it will be hard enough to silence him if he once begins to talk; but don't speak, just now, Bessie—I want to hear what will come next."

"We will prove," said Mr. Calendar, "that the service of the summons and complaint was, in every instance, made by this boy, unless the fact is admitted, and we will follow it up by proving that he is not twenty-one years of age."

"You can't do it, squire," said the justice; "that dodge has been tried before now, and it won't work. No defendant has ever been able to make out that that boy is under twenty-one."

"But has any one ever been able to make out

that he is *over* twenty-one?" asked Mr. Calendar.

"That ain't the pint, squire," said the justice; "I take it the law presumes every one to be of lawful age until the contrary appears, and the contrary doesn't appear. The court knows this boy, and his uncle being the constable and having but one leg, he can't serve summonses when there's any call to be spry, so this here boy is deputized, and he does it, and it's the law of this court that he is of lawful age, and that makes it lawful; and what's more, Squire Calendar, as I have to tell them that practises here, which you don't, a defendant in this court who has got a defense had better put it in, and not go fooling round on technicalities. If you are into a court, what odds does it make how you got into it? So jine issue, squire, if you are going to jine, and if not I'll enter judgment."

"Very well," said Mr. Calendar, good-naturedly, "if such is the law of the court, I must bow to it, and all I can do is to put in a written plea to the jurisdiction; alleging the fact that the summons was served by a minor, and then I will offer to prove the fact. This will save all our rights on appeal."

He sat down to prepare the plea. The silence
9

which followed for a moment was broken by a crimson-nosed, irascible old lawyer, long since re tired from practice, who had hobbled into the court-room and seated himself close to the bench, determined to enjoy the legal tilt to the utmost of his capacity.   Mr. Calendar's plea to the juris-diction delighted him; and he turned to the jus-tice and growled out his satisfaction.

"Calendar has got you, judge; there will be a *venire de novo* sure."

"Sam, Sam," said Bessie, shocked at an inter-ruption which the justice disregarded; "what is that awful old man saying; is it any thing disre-spectful to papa?"

"No," said Sam, "it is something disrespect-ful to Justice Hazey."

"Well, do tell me what *venire de* something means.   Oh, dear! I wish I wasn't so ignorant."

"It means a rap over the knuckles by a higher court to a lower court, and that is what lower courts are getting all the time, and what old red nose there thinks this court will get, and so do I."

"What a queer queer thing law is!" solilo-quized Bessie.

But Justice Hazey's court was not doomed to experience the predicted rap over the knuckles.

Mr. Limber had interrupted the preparation of Mr. Calendar's plea by a hurried whisper, and, after a brief consultation with his client, the lawyer quietly dropped his pen, and, without rising, said to the justice that Mr. Limber preferred to raise no question as to the service. He would therefore waive that point and put in a general denial, and let the overseers of the poor produce their witnesses, and prove their case, if they could. He should be very glad to have them show, by competent testimony, the actual value of the bran and sawdust, and other particles which figured so largely in the complaint, and, in order to relieve his honor from the responsibility of deciding so difficult a question of fact, he demanded a jury.

The testy old lawyer was thoroughly disgusted at this sudden extinction of Mr. Calendar's plea.

" Why, Calendar, what a fool you are! Why don't you go to the country, without waiving your plea to the jurisdiction ? "

" Dear Sam," said Bessie, trembling with alarm, " is that old man crazy ? He is talking in the wildest way; what does he mean by telling Mr. Calendar to go to the country, when he and all of us are in the country now ? "

"Going to the country, Bess, is a law-term for submitting a case to a jury."

"That is the queerest thing yet," said Bessie; "why do they call it going to the country?"

"Because," said Sam, "when your case goes to a jury, you are literally 'all abroad.'"

"If you want a jury, Squire Calendar," said the justice, proud of his triumph, but very glad of the opportunity of getting rid of the case for the present, "I will summon one, and the case will stand adjourned to this day week."

But Mr. Limber again whispered to Mr. Calendar, and with increased earnestness of manner. After a few minutes' delay, Mr. Calendar rose and said, with his imperturbable smile, that however perfect his defense in law and in fact, he was of course bound to obey implicitly his client's instructions, and these were to waive a jury, and indeed to waive every defense. "Mr. Limber," he continued, "declines to contest the suit, and desires me to say, that he admits all the facts stated in the complaint, and is ready to pay the penalty, or, rather, the sum of two hundred dollars—the largest sum for which the justice could give judgment."

There was a general movement and murmur

of surprise. The relieved boy took a big bite of his apple. Justice Hazey, with great alacrity, wrote " Settled," in large letters on the summons, while the abusive old lawyer growled out :

" What a pack of fools ! why, Calendar, that's a *felo de se.*"

" Sam, dear," said Bessie, " what is a *felo de se ?* "

" A fellow who commits suicide, and that is what papa has gone and done," replied Sam, who could not conceal his disappointment and chagrin at this unexpected surrender to the enemy.

" O Sam, what do you mean ? "

" I mean he has cut his own throat, but figuratively, Bess, of course—don't start so—you can see he is bleeding now."

" Oh, if you mean papa is paying the money, I understand it ; dear me, if paying will only end this dreadful law business, I shall be only too happy. But, Sam, what is Dick Folio going to do now ? "

Dick Folio was going to do a very popular thing. As Mr. Limber counted out the two hundred dollars, he rose and said that of course this prompt settlement ended the case against Mr. Limber, and no judgment need be entered ; so far as the costs were concerned, he preferred to

waive them.   Then, raising his voice, and looking
round upon the audience, he added that he was
prepared to do the same in every case in which
the defendant would pay the penalty.   The cost
of printing the papers he should wish to collect,
as the *Freebooter* office had kept its men at work
nearly all night, and this expense, though not
taxable, ought to be provided for, but, beyond
this actual outlay, he would relinquish all the
costs if, by so doing, he could, at a personal sac-
rifice, aid in bringing an unpleasant matter to a
satisfactory conclusion."

The general effect of this little speech was
very favorable, but the irate old lawyer was now
trebly disgusted.

" Why, Folio, I thought you had some sense.
What a goose you are to throw away your costs !
You ought to be thrown over the bar.   It's five
dollars by statute in every case, and an execution
against the person ; you can have the money, or
a *cepi corpus*, sure."

" Dear, dear, Sam ! " whispered Bessie, now
thoroughly alarmed, " who is *cepi corpus*—is it
law Latin for undertaker, and will Dick Folio be
killed if they throw him over the bar; is it a very
high bar?   O Sam, Sam, I shall die if I stay
here any longer."

"*Cepi corpus*," said Sam, laughing, "isn't a person, though old Sheriff Pounder thought so, and used to say that he had searched all through the county for him ever since he was sheriff, without finding him anywhere. It means bail or jail, and perhaps jail anyhow."

"What gibberish you talk! but about throwing Dick Folio over the bar, or whatever it is, will he be hurt?"

"No, no, Bess, that's all metaphorical. A lawyer is thrown over the bar when he gets too wicked to practise in court with all the other lawyers."

"I should hardly think any one could ever get so wicked as that," said Bessie, very innocently.

By this time the two hundred dollars had been paid and receipted for, and Justice Hazey was beginning to be in mortal fear lest he should have something to decide in the next case, when Mr. Calendar again took the floor and begged to express his appreciation of the liberal and generous offer of his learned young friend Mr. Folio, and to say further that while "All's well that ends well" was not exactly a legal maxim, unless indeed Lord Bacon, and not Shakespeare, was entitled to the credit of originating it, it rarely received a happier application than when lawsuits were settled and lawyers dispensed with. Having finished this little preface, Mr. Calendar went on to say that he had great satisfaction in announcing the further instructions he had just received from his client, Mr. Limber, who proposed, as the penalties for which the other ninety-nine defendants were sued, were all incurred at his own house, and in the course of an entertainment intended to contribute only to the pleasure of those who participated in it, to pay the penalty himself in every case, together with the expense of printing to which Mr. Folio had alluded, and he was ready to pay the money on the spot.

There was a general burst of applause. Inwardly, Justice Hazey was delighted, and visions of a third term floated before his fancy. Outwardly, he hammered on his desk, and reminded his audience again that they were in a court-room, and not at a town-meeting. The abusive old lawyer was in a fourfold rage.

"Why, Limber, you are the biggest fool in Spindle. Do you want me to sue out a writ *de lunatico?*"

"Sam," said Bessie, with fresh alarm, "what under the sun is a writ *de lunatico?*"

"It is a way the courts have of writing a man down an ass at the request of his friends and relatives, but which old red-nose there seems to think papa has done without any assistance."

" I wish they would take the old wretch out of the court-room; he is a perfect torment. But, Sam, who is this that is going to speak now. I declare if it isn't Mr. Bender."

It was indeed Mr. Bender, who, upon the conclusion of Mr. Calendar's remarks, had forced his way from a position near the door, where, in company with a friend, he was obscurely nursing a newly-lighted cigar, to the table in front of the justice. He was evidently greatly excited, and not a little embarrassed; but he was bent on discharging his mind. Mr. Calendar and Mr. Folio politely made way for him, while the boy silently stole away at his approach, and took a safe position on the side of the table nearest the justice, with his eye on the inkstand, and his heart, as well as his apple, in his mouth.

" Judge—your honor— " said Mr. Bender, " I am entered here, so to speak, as a defendant, and and it is my intention to come to time—as always —when called." Here Mr. Bender deposited his hat and gloves and cigar on the table with great deliberation, also his cane; after doing which, he divested himself of his overcoat, adjusted his crimson necktie, and continued as follows:

"I suppose, judge—your honor—fair play is a jewel, even if you are in a court-room, and whatever is rulable I abide by, and the referee's decision, or judge's, or umpire's, as the case may be, all of which your honor is or are, so to speak —and I did suppose and others—as this being a general entry of all weights and ages against the overseers, we would pool our pleas or defenses, so to speak—which your honor well understands though not exactly expressed in legal forms—but while waiting for the call and ready for a fair start—here comes Mr. Limber and pays forfeit, and, so to speak, withdraws the whole ninety-and-nine entries, colts, fillies, and all, and the overseers not so much as called, and optional with them to walk over the course. Now the ring is the same as the turf: if a man's seconds or backers throw up the sponge, all right ; but so long as he comes to the scratch and time not up, the same as I and other defendants here, there is no such thing as giving the stakes to the other side, and what we want, judge—your honor—so to speak —is to throw up our own sponges when whipped and not before, and not to be jockeyed out of our defenses. Now, judge, I put into the raffle, which I believe was drawn regular and on the square, not being present myself, but a friend

took it in my name, likewise in his own, in aid of
charity—also persuaded by a young lady—but
seemingly some one has gone back on us, age and
weight unknown—and now comes the poor overseers and say it's all against the law—which we
supposed as between man and man and the community in general was—so to speak—a dead
letter, but says you .the Revived Statues have
brought it to life and set it a-going—supposing
it can be set a-going by boys which Mr. Calendar says it cannot being infants, but Mr. Limber
waives the boy; so then if I have had my chance
in the raffle and the consequence is I must cover
my card here, so to speak, with ten dollars, why,
judge, your honor, it's my own ten dollars I want
to pay and not another man's, and if it comes to
that let each one pay his own score, say I, and
pay it in cash, and if it goes to the poor where's
the odds?"

Here Mr. Bender stopped short, and sat down
suddenly, in the seat vacated by the wary boy, in
the midst of a burst of applause which the justice vainly tried to hammer into silence. Mr.
Bender's speech had proved a word in season,
whether fitly spoken or not. It turned the tide
of public opinion, and gave a new impulse to the
ninety-nine who hitherto had thought only of

avoiding their liability. Defendants who had
come to plead now wanted to remain to pay.
The doctrine that every man should pay his own
score, and pay it in cash, so forcibly put by Mr.
Bender, was accepted as heartily as if it had
been a new discovery instead of an old truth set
in a new light.

But now David Limber was on his feet again,
waving his hand in a deprecatory way, and evidently meaning to be heard. He was not a man
of fluent speech, but, knowing what he wanted,
and being bent on carrying his point, he was as
good an orator for the occasion as ever Brutus
was, or Mark Antony, or even Mr. Bender.

"My friends," said he, quite forgetting that
whoever was entitled to the last word, Justice
Hazey was entitled to the first, "I agree with
Mr. Bender that every one should pay his own
score, and the reason why I insist on paying all
these penalties is simply that they are my score,
and no other man's. As Mr. Calendar has said,
the raffle was in my house, and you were all
there on my invitation. Now, in old times, as
we have read in books, and perhaps some one
here, in his younger days, may have seen, when,
late at night, a party of good fellows would lock
the doors and drink their toasts, they had a wild

way of throwing their glasses over their shoulders and letting them break on the floor. I don't believe any of them got a bill next day from their host for broken glass. Now, you came to my house to have a merry time, and it seems while you were there you broke the law. Well, that's my affair, not yours, the same as if I had set you at a game of blind-man's-buff instead of the raffle, and you had run against a mirror or a vase and broken it, instead of running against the Revised Statutes and breaking them. What is done under my own roof, by my own guests, is my loss, and I must bear it. And besides, I might have known, and perhaps I did know, you were running just this risk, and, if I let it go on, who else should stand in the gap? One thing you may take my word for, no one has done anything mean in setting the overseers against you, as Mr. Bender seems to think. They could not have done differently, and they need this money for a new hospital for our poor, and it's a thing I've long had in mind to do, and if I do it in this way it isn't paying your debts, but only giving a Christmas-present to the poor; and, for the chance to do it, I owe you all my thanks."

Mr. Limber's tone and manner showed plainly that he meant every word he said, and it would not do to disappoint him. Mr. Bender was shaken, but not convinced. He had lost breath in his long speech, and, after Mr. Limber's rejoinder, he was by no means certain of his ground, though he had no idea of giving it up. But, before he could get on his feet or say a word, Mr. Folio jumped up and informed the court that, while Mr. Limber was speaking, Mr. Calendar had passed over to him his client's check for the nine hundred and ninety-nine dollars, and had settled with him for the expenses, so that all the penalties were paid and the suits ended, and the overseers had no claim against any one.

Mr. Bender had just recovered his breath. "Is that rulable?" he began; but the justice was having a word with Mr. Calendar, and paid no heed to the question.

The irascible old lawyer, who felt that he had been cheated out of his day's sport, answered it for him. "Rulable? yes—with such a nest of ninnies; put up your money, Bender, and it will be the most sensible thing that has been done in this court-room to-day.

"Then must I let another man pay my forfeit?" said Mr. Bender, trying to work himself into a passion.

"Yes," said the old lawyer, "its *damnum absque injuria.*"

"Dear Sam," said Bessie, "that dreadful old man is beginning to swear. Why does the judge allow it? The constable ought to put him out."

"He is very much put out as it is," said Sam; "but, Bess, he wasn't swearing—that was some more of his law Latin."

"It sounded very profane. What did it all mean?"

"It meant that people are sometimes more frightened than hurt, and that is the condition of Mr. Bender, and all these other ninety-and-nine, thanks to papa."

"Sam," said Bessie, after a moment's pause, "isn't papa perfectly splendid?"

"He has paid out a lot of money," said Sam, thoughtfully.

"For all that," said Bessie, "it is gorgeous—oh, I do want to kiss papa ever so much!"

"There is nothing to hinder," said Sam; "everybody is going away and we will go too, and let mamma know how this has turned out."

Bessie was by her father's side in a moment, and her arms were around his neck. David Limber was a hero to his daughter, and she wanted to give him an ovation. Her feeling was largely shared by many others, who thronged around him and were loud in their expressions of satisfaction at the unlooked-for turn which his liberality had given to the proceedings of the day.

Mr. Calendar waited for the excitement to subside, and then said to his client, in the hearing of Mr. Bender, who seemed half disposed to remonstrate against the injustice which he had suffered :

" You have had your own way, Limber, as you generally do, and I congratulate you. There is one thing you must see to in order to vindicate the majesty of the law. There is a section of the statute which I did not read to you, declaring all raffling contracts void, so that the winner is not entitled to the prize. She may have her dollar back, but not the doll. Tell Mrs. Limber this. I think you told me the girl had gone away."

" Yes, and the doll is in Mrs. Limber's custody."

" By all means let her keep it safely ; it would be a thousand pities if she slipped through your fingers now."

" Come with me, Calendar, and take your dinner with us, and explain this and all the rest to my wife. I want Folio, too," and Mr. Limber hurried to arrest the successful attorney for the overseers, who was descending the steps with Sam, and vainly endeavoring to answer the questions with which he was plying him.

Mr. Bender lingered with his friend in the precincts of the temple of justice. He was in an uncomfortable frame of mind. The ten-dollar note which he had taken from his pocket as he closed his address, for the purpose of paying his score, and which the old lawyer had advised him to put up again, was twisted around the forefinger of his right hand and he looked at it with an uneasy expression. He was the last man to quit the court-house. He paused in the vestibule to relight his cigar, saying to his companion as he did so—

"I've half a mind to light it with this greenback; let's go to the Shades and take a drink."

The Spindle Shades, although a tippling-house and justly under the ban of reputable society, was a comparatively decent and quiet place of resort, frequented by a better class of drinkers than those who haunted the lower dram-shops of Spindle. Mr. Bender and his friend were evidently not chance customers, and a certain degree of familiarity with their tastes was exhibited by the bar-tender, as he anticipated their wants in a manner satisfactory to both.

10

"Been to court?" asked the bar-tender as the empty glasses were set down.

"Just come from there," said Mr. Bender, "and you don't catch me in another. It's a kind of game where an honest sport has no chance."

"I can tell you something that likely you don't know," said the bar-keeper, polishing the surface of his counter; "that church doll, as they call it, belongs here and is a-coming here."

"How is that?" said Mr. Bender, with evident surprise and no little curiosity.

"Just this way. It was won in the raffle by Bridget Looney, Mrs. Looney that is, you know, Pat's wife, and she writes a letter from New York, it's Pat's writing be sure, and he was always a bit of a scholar, and her name is signed to it, and she gives the doll over to the Spindle Shades; and this morning the letter came, and the boss has sent two of us up to Limber's to fetch it. They'll be here pretty soon."

"What do you want of a doll here?" said Mr. Bender.

"Why, you see it's 'Pat Looney's luck,' they call it, for his number carried it off from all the big folks, and Pat promised it and his wife to set it up here as a kind of memory-piece, seeing he's gone away for good; and we are going to put it just here," said the bar-tender, pointing to a wooden shelf projecting from the base of the mirror behind him, a bad eminence on which Centuria might rest, her form reflected at full length in the polished surface at her back, with transient glimpses of her face and front in the silver-plated mountings of the ale-pumps at her feet, flanked on either side by the tall glasses whose reversed bases supported lemons of enormous size, while brilliant tankards and colored bottles of various hues formed a resplendent pyramid, on whose apex she would seem to stand or soar.

"Pat Looney's luck!" sneered Mr. Bender; "she has brought bad luck to whoever has had to do with her."

"Not to Pat," said the bar-tender, as he swept his cloth over the smooth surface of his counter, for a final polish, "he always comes out ahead; bless you, if he was run for guv'ner he'd be elected. He is up for Assemblyman now, and sure to win."

"Who has gone for the doll?" asked Mr. Bender, twirling the still unpocketed bank-note in his fingers.

"The twins. They were sitting around here and the boss gave them the letter, and they started half an hour ago. It's a bit of a walk cut to Limber's and back."

" The twins " was the familiar designation of
a couple of good-for-naughts, in no way related
to each other, except by the natural tie of depravity, who made the Spindle Shades their head-
quarters, and were proud of being regarded as
its most faithful allies.

" Mr. Bender, without a word further, paid
his reckoning and left the place. When he gained
the street he paused, took a few slowly-drawn
whiffs of his cigar, and then said to his companion, in a solemn tone:

" It's my judgment these fellows are not entitled to that doll. The raffle is broke up by law,
the forfeits paid, the stakes can't be paid over.
It ain't rulable. There's no law for it."

" What's all that to you ? " said his friend.
" Haven't you had law enough about that blessed
raffle ? "

" Yes," said Mr. Bender, " too much law and
no justice. Come along, and we will make things
right yet. You and I can meet these precious
twins half-way, and take the doll from them and
return it to the owner. Pat Looney's wife has
no right to it, no more than you or I. She can
have her dollar, but not the doll ; these were
Squire Calendar's very words, and I'll swear to
them."

"I heard all that," said his friend, "but what gives you the right to take it away from them that has it ? It will be grand larceny, or assault and battery, and that boy or somebody will be after you, sharp."

Mr. Bender untwisted the greenback, and folded it so as to display its figures.

"Seems to me," said he, "as though this ten dollars was owing to some one, I don't know who. When we meet the twins, we'll tell them the raffle is off, and they've got stolen property in hand, and it'll be six months in the county jail for each of them, and they had better get rid of it, and take ten dollars in exchange, and who should ever know that they got the doll, if they have got it, seeing there's no right to have it ? Come on," repeated Mr. Bender, as the success of his project seemed all the clearer from his lucid statement of it.

"But there's a lady in the case," urged his cautious friend, "even if her name is Bridget."

"The lady in the case," said Mr. Bender, "is Mrs. Limber. You may come or not, as you please, but I am going. I'll see justice done. Oh, you are coming. Well, we are on the home-stretch now and a clear field."

CHAPTER X.

APOTHEOSIS OF CENTURIA.

Mrs. Limber had ample opportunity, after the departure of her husband and children for the court-house, to review the checkered course of events which had its origin in the ill-fated raffle. She saw, clearly enough, that her husband's warning voice, even though it was but an echo of Mr. Proser's bodements, might better have been heeded. At the same time she found consolation in the purity of her intentions in behalf of St. Parvus, and in the certainty that no human being, not even Mr. Proser himself, could have foreseen that the horrid monster of litigation, now stalking through the peaceful homes of Spindle, would have been evoked, as by some wicked enchantment, from her innocent scheme. The closing scenes of the fair were an abiding source of discomfort. She had parted from her friend Mrs. Chancel, if not in anger, at least in irritation, and she felt that this too was partly due to her own want of candor. She had not dealt fairly with her friend. The more she reflected the more vexed she became with herself, and, at last, yielding to a sudden impulse, she resolved to go at once to Mrs. Chancel, and tell her the whole story of Pat Looney's luck and Bridget's dire revenge, so that, whatever might be the issue of the trial, she should be at peace with her friend.

A dozen steps from her gate she encountered Mrs. Chancel herself. A corresponding stress of emotions, and the pressure of self-reproach for her parting sarcasm, and, even more than these, the spur of new and startling discoveries, had driven her from the rectory to Mrs. Limber. The two friends embraced each other, and the shadow of their misunderstanding was lost in the sunshine of a cordial greeting, renewed in Mrs. Limber's parlor, with fresh demonstrations of affection, unhindered by furs and wraps. The two ladies seated themselves, side by side, on a sofa before the fire, and Mrs. Chancel, as her manner was, began the conversation.

"So it is your husband, my dear, who has gone and turned State's evidence, and given all this information to the overseers of the poor, and got himself, and you, and all of us sued. It is his latest invention, and surely the newest, if not the most useful. I never imagined he was such a genius!"

Mrs. Limber looked unutterable ignorance and unmistakable curiosity.

"You must know, then; and, of course, there was no way of your guessing it before, that Mr. Limber has been to the rectory this morning, and confessed all to Mr. Chancel."

"All what?" gasped Mrs. Limber.

"All this," said Mrs. Chancel, "that, after he saw we were fully bent and determined on the raffle—and you know, dear, we were fully bent and determined on it—and after he had been to my husband to get him to stop it, and he, poor man, couldn't exactly grasp the subject, as he says, then Mr. Limber went to John Calendar, and, without letting him into any of his plans, got from him all the law about raffles and lotteries out of the Revised Statutes and the constitution, and I don't know how many more musty law-books, all mixed up with John Calendar's crotchets, I suppose. And then came Mr. Limber's grand invention; having made the discovery that the overseers of the poor could sue everybody concerned in the raffle, he devised the plan of having everybody sued, himself included;

then, to show that it was all his doing, and no
one's else, he made Mr. Calendar give him a receipted bill, with the date, so that, if need be, he
could prove that this was all planned before the
raffle, and then off he went to Huge Boulder, as
the boys call him, the head-man of the overseers
of the poor, and showed him the law, and told
him that if the new hospital was ever to be built,
here was the way to get the money, and you
may be sure he jumped at it, and so did they all.
Mr. Calendar was their lawyer, but he mistrusted
what your husband was about, and wrote to the
overseers of the poor to employ Dick Folio, if
they had any suits to bring. So Dick was the
attorney, and your husband contrived that he
should buy the subscription-list, so as to make
sure of the names, and so as to have the papers
all printed at night, and everybody caught next
morning, as they were, all but Bridget Looney;
and then, last of all, and best of all, what does
he do, after letting every one fret and fume for a
week, but come into court and pay all the penalties out of his own pocket, just as he told Mr.
Chancel, early this morning, he meant to do, and
he has paid the balance of the church debt besides, and he means to pay whatever more the
hospital may cost, though that is a secret, and

all this is Mr. Limber's Christmas-present to the poor of Spindle!"

"It is just like him," burst out Mrs. Limber, her eyes as full as her heart. Then she began to cry with all her might.

Up to that moment Mrs. Chancel had not thought of such a thing as crying over this good news, but she could not resist the contagion, and her tears flowed faster than her friend's.

Mrs. Limber suddenly stopped crying.

"I declare we are two fools. He has made you and me and all of us ridiculous. Dear me! what shall we do with these husbands?"

"After all," said Mrs Chancel, with dry eyes, "isn't it just a little bit nearer the truth that we have made ourselves ridiculous?"

"Perhaps so," said Mrs. Limber; "and that is ever so much better than being made ridiculous by anybody else."

"Another thing, my dear," said Mrs Chancel, "your husband has converted Mr. Chancel entirely. He says we and he were all wrong, and Mr. Limber was all right, that the raffle never ought to have been, and that he should have interfered and broken it up when he was applied to. He is perfectly in love with Mr. Limber. Do you

know, I think what won his heart was his coming, as it were, to confessional."

"But," said Mrs. Limber, "I thought you
said just now that Mr. Chancel confessed he was
all wrong, and Mr. Limber was all right."

"Oh, dear, yes, but he only confessed to me—
husband to wife—and that is a kind of confession,
you know, which even Presbyterians believe in."

"At all events," said Mrs. Limber, "confess-
ing one to another is Scriptural, and I have a
confession to make to you. I was coming to
make it when we met at my gate;" and then
Mrs. Limber unburdened her conscience and told
the whole story of her encounter with Bridget,
and of the subsequent plots and machinations of
that unblushing bride.

"I never felt easy about the raffle," said Mrs.
Limber, "from the moment of my scene with
Bridget; but who could have dreamed of what
has happened?"

"Who, indeed?" chimed in Mrs. Chancel;
"but, my dear child," she suddenly exclaimed,
looking in the direction of the front-windows,
which opened to the floor, "what in the world
are those two men coming here for?" and in
great alarm she pointed out what seemed to her
the worst-looking couple she had ever seen in

Spindle. The truth is, that daylight was particularly unbecoming to the twins, who, like many fashionable young ladies, looked their worst in the morning, and, as they reconnoitred the premises with an aggressive air, intent on their mission as the escort of Centuria to the Shades, the two ladies were on the brink of a panic.

"What shall we do?" cried Mrs. Chancel; "are there no men in the house?"

Mrs. Limber hurriedly closed the inside shutters and rang the bell. She then ran to fasten the chain of the front-door, but it had so chanced that when the two ladies entered the house they had inadvertently left the door unlatched, and the wind had opened it, so that, as the mistress of the mansion stepped into the hall, she found herself face to face with the invaders. They had paused on the door-step, and taken an attitude sufficiently pacific and respectful to disarm any suspicion that they were the common enemies of mankind. Both were smoking, but it was evidently the pipe of peace whose odors were wafted toward Mrs. Limber, as she received the salutations which were tendered her. One of the two made a slight advance, holding forth a letter, which Mrs. Limber, with a spasm of courage, actually took.

At this juncture, the housemaid appeared in answer to the bell, and motioning to her to remain on guard, Mrs. Limber reëntered the parlor, wondering at her own daring, and exciting the equal wonder of Mrs. Chancel by exhibiting the letter of which she had been made the recipient. It was addressed to Mrs. Limber, and under the concentrated gaze of her own eyes, and those of Mrs. Chancel, its contents were soon disclosed as follows :

New York, *December* 15, 18—.

Mrs. David Limber :

If my chance wins, it is number 63, and Miss Bessie has my money, please will you deliver the doll to the gentleman which brings this, it is in full of all demands, and it is a free Christmas gift to the Spindle Shades from me and Pat, which he sends his respects, baring no malice, and I am the same, no more at present, from your friend,

Bridget Looney.

"Oh, get it, get it quick!" said Mrs. Limber. "No, stay here and I will go for it."

"Let me go," said Mrs. Chancel, who saw that any reopening of the raffle gave a new shock to Mrs. Limber's nerves. "Where is it?"

"In my cedar-closet, on the top shelf, right-hand side, in a paper box. The key is in the basket on the bureau in my bedroom. I shall only be too, too glad when it is out of the house."

Mrs. Chancel mounted the stairs, found the key and the box, and with her own hands delivered Centuria to the twins. She thought of the murderers in the Tower and of the babes in the wood, and of all the braces of stage-villains she had ever read of or heard of or seen, and shuddered at her own temerity. It never occurred to her to appreciate the involuntary tribute which the two scamps paid to her sex, in receiving the package from her, without scrutiny or question, never doubting that a lady, such as she, was to be trusted with implicit faith.

The envoys of the winning, if not the winsome bride, took their departure, wholly unconscious of the terror with which they had inspired the ladies, and of the admiration they had excited in the housemaid, who followed their retreating footsteps with her eyes, and with a tender regret that the rapid movements of Mrs. Chancel had nipped in the bud an acquaintance which had progressed no further than the preliminary stages of two winks and a double blush.

The door had been closed for about half an hour on Centuria and her new custodians, when

Mr. Limber, Sam, and Bessie, accompanied by
Mr. Calendar, Dick Folio, and the rector, whom
they had overtaken in their rapid walk from the
court-house, mounted the steps. Mrs. Limber
had recovered from the shock of her last encounter, sufficiently to be in readiness for a meet-
ing to which her husband had looked forward
with no little uneasiness. The presence of Mrs.
Chancel at once assured him that his wife knew
all, the smiles which greeted him augured well,
and in an instant all doubts were dispelled, as her
arms were thrown around his neck, and he heard
her saying, her voice broken by a succession of
little sobs and little kisses, "Do forgive me,
dear husband, and—and, I will forgive you."

David Limber was a man of few words and
few kisses. He gave his wife a hearty hug, and
sat down beside her on the sofa. It was mani-
fest that, whoever was to forgive, and whatever
was to be forgiven, the transaction was complete.

While this little interlude was in progress,
Mrs. Chancel had been engaged in questioning
the new-comers as to the incidents of the trial.
Mr. Limber interrupted a graphic description
which Dick Folio was giving to his wife of Justice Hazey's proceedings, by repeating Mr. Cal-

endar's injunction to keep possession of the doll.

"You must see to it, Martha, that it is not given up to Bridget Looney. The raffle was illegal and void. She is to have her money back but not the doll; so be sure that she does not get it."

"But she has got it already," shrieked Mrs. Limber. "It is but just now, two dreadful, desperate men came and demanded it, and took it away. What could we do? We were alone in the house with the women. Oh, dear! I am the most wretched creature alive. Is there to be no end to my misery?"

"Two men are not Bridget," said Sam; "we know that she is away and cannot be found."

"They had her written order," said Mrs. Chancel, producing it as she spoke.

Sam took the letter and read it aloud. "It is plain enough, said he, as he folded it again, "Centuria has gone to the Spindle Shades. She is a trophy of the luck of the Looneys. She will be metamorphosed into a divinity of drinks."

"What a cruel apotheosis for a Christian doll," cried Mrs. Chancel, "and to think that I gave her with my own hands!"

"But it was all my fault," sobbed Mrs. Limber.

A sudden outcry from Bessie, who had turned to the window to hide her vexation, broke in upon her mother's lament.

"Are they coming again?" groaned Mrs. Chancel, before whose mental vision the twins were in constant view.

"No, but Mr. Bender and another man are coming, and I do believe they are bringing Centuria back. Oh, it is too good to be true, but at all events they have got the box.—Run, Sam! oh, if it should be empty after all!"

Sam was at the street-door in an instant. He threw it wide open. Mr. Bender and his friend —conquering heroes evidently—made a triumphal entry into the parlor and deposited their burden on the centre-table. No fears now that the box was empty. It was plain enough that there had been a rescue, and the good news, beaming from every part of Mr. Bender's rosy face, hardly-needed his confirmatory announcement: "There is the stakes, and the bets if any are all off."

There was a general chorus of applause as the cover was removed from the box, and the assurance of Centuria's deliverance from the base uses to which she had been destined by the house of Looney was made doubly sure by the sight

11

of her waxen face and untarnished Parisian costume.

"Tell us all about it," cried Bessie to Mr.
Bender, who was her second hero of the day, and,
thus solicited, that gentleman, with modest pride,
described his outraged feelings when he heard,
during his momentary visit to the Spindle Shades,
of the fate which was impending over Centuria,
and his sudden resolve that justice should be
done by her summary recapture and restoration
to Mrs. Limber, and how he had successfully
achieved this result by a little strategy and the
outlay of the ten dollars which he had succeeded
in paying as his score, in spite of Mr. Limber.

"This crowns the day," said Mr. Limber, brim-
ful of satisfaction. "Mr. Bender and his friend
must join us at dinner; you are all my guests, I
cannot spare one."

Sam was not entirely at ease; he turned to
Mr. Calendar with an anxious look, and the question—

"May they not attempt to replevy her?"

"Dear Sam," said Bessie, "what do you mean,
you are as bad as that awful old man at the court-
house. What is it to replevy a thing? Is it
anything dreadful?"

"It is a kind of grab-game, which you play at

with sheriffs and coroners," said Sam. "If Bridget Looney replevies the doll, she will send the sheriff here to claim it as her property, and he will take it off; and then we can send the coroner after the sheriff and take it back as our property; and then—"

"Sam!" broke in Mrs. Limber, "is this going to end in a coroner's inquest? Is there to be a *post mortem* over this poor victim of the law? Dear me! what shall we do with these lawyers?"

"No," said Mr. Calendar, "this is the end. Bridget Looney cannot replevy because she never had any legal ownership. The doll belongs to the original owner."

"And who is the original owner?" asked Sam.

"I should say Mrs. Chancel," said Mrs. Limber. "She is the owner, it was her doll."

"And I," said Mrs. Chancel, "should say Mrs. Limber, for I gave the doll to her."

"But it was given for a purpose which has failed," said Sam.

"Not at all," said the rector; "the church has received her full value."

"Oh, dear!" sighed Bessie, "here is another dreadful trouble. It is going to be impossible to find an owner for Centuria."

"It is a pure question of law," observed Mr. Folio, sententiously; "why not leave it to Mr. Calendar's decision?"

"There is no precedent to guide me," said Mr. Calendar, "unless our good friend the rector finds one in the judgment of Solomon. We might divide Centuria, and give one half to Mrs. Limber and the other half to Mrs. Chancel."

"Oh, no, no!" cried both ladies at once.

"It would be very easy to settle this," said Mr. Bender, "by a toss up, heads or tails, but, says you, there's the Revived Statues again, and where are we?"

"Allow me to make a suggestion," said Mr. Calendar. "Centuria has been rescued from the bar-room by the ingenuity and courage of our friend Mr. Bender; let her be enshrined in the hospital."

"By all means," exclaimed Mr. Limber; "it is her just due. She is its real founder, and she shall have a niche in the main entrance."

"It will be a charming symbol," said Mr. Chancel; "she will represent the angel of charity with her wings clipped by the sword of justice."

"Justice Hazey," suggested Sam, in a stage whisper, which luckily the rector did not hear and which Mrs. Chancel forgave.

"She will perpetuate Mr. Bender's gallantry," said Mr. Limber.

"And Mr. Folio's legal victory," said Mr. Calendar.

"And Mr. Limber's benevolence," said Mrs. Chancel.

"And my folly," said Mrs. Limber.

"And its surprisingly good results," said Mrs. Chancel. "If folly pays church debts and builds hospitals, it seems like a very good substitute for wisdom."

"Not folly, after all," said Mrs. Limber, "but folly well punished and well forgiven."

She took the rector's arm and led the way to dinner.

Dick Folio and Bessie lingered in the bay-window of the parlor, and were late in taking their places at the dinner-table. What passed between them during that brief interview does not concern our story, but the young lawyer has been heard to declare that the best outcome of Mrs. Limber's raffle was the winning for himself of a lawful prize in the lottery of life.

"One thing is certain," said David Limber at the close of an evening spent with Mr. Calendar over the plans for the new hospital, which, as it grew toward completion, grew also in the proportions of its founder's liberality, and made his Christmas-gift a lasting memorial of his name—"one thing is certain, we may have many strange experiences, there may be strikes and floods, fires, pestilence and famine, tornadoes and earthquakes, but there will never be another raffle in Spindle, at least among decent people."

"Nor would there be anywhere else," said Mr. Calendar, "if every one were told the story of Mrs. Limber's raffle, and would lay to heart its moral, that the devil's edge-tools are sure to cut, no matter how dexterously handled by saint or sinner."

NOTE.

PAGE 67. The aiding of public objects by means of State lotteries has been, in this country, an imitation of the methods of Continental Europe and of Great Britain. Up to the year 1826, lotteries for public improvements and for benevolent purposes were authorized in England, and both the Colonial and State legislatures in America followed the example of the mother country.

To the institutions mentioned by Mr. Calendar as having been aided by public lotteries must be added Princeton College, which, strangely enough, appears to have had such help from a lottery authorized by the State of Connecticut in 1753. I have in my possession a ticket of this lottery, printed in the style of the pre-Revolutionary period. It reads as follows:

"*Connecticut* LOTTERY.

For the Benefit of the College of New Jersey.

1753 · Numb. 2495.

THIS Ticket entitles the Possessor to such *Prize* as may be drawn against its Number, (if demanded within six Months after the Drawing is finished) subject to a Deduction of 15 per Cent.

E   John Lloyd."

THE END.

BOOKS BY MRS. EVERARD COTES (Sara Jeannette Duncan).

A DAUGHTER OF TO-DAY. A novel. 12mo. Cloth, $1.50.

Few literary *débutantes* have met with the success obtained by Sara Jeannette Duncan's first book, "A Social Departure." Her succeeding books showed the same powers of quick observation and graphic description, the same ability to identify and portray types. Meantime, the author has greatly enlarged her range of experience and knowledge of the world A true cosmopolite, London, Paris, and Calcutta have become familiar to her, as well as New York and Montreal. The title of her new book is no misnomer, and the author's vigorous treatment of her theme has given us a book distinguished not only by acute study of character, command of local color, and dramatic force, but also by contemporaneous interest.

THE SIMPLE ADVENTURES OF A MEMSAHIB. With 37 Illustrations by F. H. TOWNSEND. 12mo. Cloth, $1.50.

"It is impossible for Sara Jeannette Duncan to be otherwise than interesting. Whether it be a voyage around the world, or an American girl's experiences in London society, or the adventures pertaining to the establishment of a youthful couple in India, there is always an atmosphere, a quality, a charm, peculiarly her own."—*Brooklyn Standard-Union.*

A SOCIAL DEPARTURE: How Orthodocia and I Went Round The World by Ourselves. With 111 Illustrations by F. H. TOWNSEND. 12mo. Paper, 75 cents; cloth, $1.75.

"Widely read and praised on both sides of the Atlantic and Pacific, with scores of illustrations which fit the text exactly and show the mind of artist and writer in unison."—*New York Evening Post*

"It is to be doubted whether another book can be found so thoroughly amusing from beginning to end."—*Boston Daily Advertiser.*

AN AMERICAN GIRL IN LONDON. With 80 Illustrations by F. H. TOWNSEND. 12mo. Paper, 75 cents; cloth, $1.50.

"One of the most naïve and entertaining books of the season."—*New York Observer.*

"So sprightly a book as this, on life in London as observed by an American, has never before been written."—*Philadelphia Bulletin.*

"Overrunning with cleverness and good will."—*New York Commercial Advertiser.*

New York: D. APPLETON & CO., 72 Fifth Avenue.

ON THE PLANTATION. By JOEL CHANDLER HARRIS, author of "Uncle Remus." With 23 Illustrations by E. W. KEMBLE, and Portrait of the Author. 12mo. Cloth, $1.50.

"The book is in the characteristic vein which has made the author so famous and popular as an interpreter of plantation character."—*Rochester Union and Advertiser.*

"Those who never tire of Uncle Remus and his stories—with whom we would be accounted—will delight in Joe Maxwell and his exploits."—*London Saturday Review.*

"Altogether a most charming book."—*Chicago Times.*

"Really a valuable, if modest, contribution to the history of the civil war within the Confederate lines, particularly on the eve of the catastrophe. Two or three new animal fables are introduced with effect; but the history of the plantation, the printing-office, the black runaways, and white deserters, of whom the impending break-up made the community tolerant, the coon and fox hunting, forms the serious purpose of the book, and holds the reader's interest from beginning to end."—*New York Evening Post.*

UNCLE REMUS: His Songs and his Sayings. The Folk-lore of the Old Plantation. By JOEL CHANDLER HARRIS. Illustrated from Drawings by F. S. CHURCH and J. H. MOSER, of Georgia. 12mo. Cloth, $1.50.

"The idea of preserving and publishing these legends, in the form in which the old plantation negroes actually tell them, is altogether one of the happiest literary conceptions of the day. And very admirably is the work done. . . . In such touches lies the charm of this fascinating little volume of legends, which deserves to be placed on a level with *Reincke Fuchs* for its quaint humor, without reference to the ethnological interest possessed by these stories, as indicating, perhaps, a common origin for very widely severed races."—*London Spectator.*

"We are just discovering what admirable literary material there is at home, what a great mine there is to explore, and how quaint and peculiar is the material which can be dug up. Mr. Harris's book may be looked on in a double light—either as a pleasant volume recounting the stories told by a typical old colored man to a child, or as a valuable contribution to our somewhat meager folk-lore. . . . To Northern readers the story of Brer (Brother—Brudder) Rabbit may be novel. To those familiar with plantation life, who have listened to these quaint old stories, who have still tender reminiscences of some good old mauma who told these wondrous adventures to them when they were children, Brer Rabbit, the Tar Baby, and Brer Fox come back again with all the past pleasures of younger days."—*New York Times.*

"Uncle Remus's sayings on current happenings are very shrewd and bright, and the plantation and revival songs are choice specimens of their sort."—*Boston Journal.*

HAND-BOOKS OF SOCIAL USAGES.

SOCIAL ETIQUETTE OF NEW YORK. Re-written and enlarged. 18mo. Cloth, gilt, $1.00.

Special pains have been taken to make this work represent accurately existing customs in New York society. The subjects treated are of visiting and visiting-cards, giving and attending balls, receptions, dinners, etc., débuts, chaperons, weddings, opera and theatre parties, costumes and customs, addresses and signatures, and funeral customs, covering so far as practicable all social usages.

DON'T; or, Directions for avoiding Improprieties in Conduct and Common Errors of Speech. By CENSOR. *Parchment-Paper Edition,* square 18mo, 30 cents. *Vest-Pocket Edition,* cloth, flexible, gilt edges, red lines, 30 cents. *Boudoir Edition* (with a new chapter designed for young people), cloth, gilt, 30 cents. 130th thousand.

"Don't" deals with manners at the table, in the drawing-room, and in public, with taste in dress, with personal habits, with common mistakes in various situations in life, and with ordinary errors of speech.

WHAT TO DO. A Companion to "Don't." By Mrs. OLIVER BELL BUNCE. Small 18mo, cloth, gilt, uniform with *Boudoir Edition* of "Don't," 30 cents.

A dainty little book, containing helpful and practical explanations of social usages and rules. It tells the reader how to entertain and how to be entertained, and it sets forth the etiquette of engagements and marriages, introductions and calls.

"GOOD FORM" IN ENGLAND. By AN AMERICAN, resident in the United Kingdom. 12mo. Cloth, $1.50.

"The *raison d'être* of this book is to provide Americans—and especially those visiting England—with a concise, comprehensive, and comprehensible hand-book which will give them all necessary information respecting 'how things are' in England.'"—*From the Preface.*

HINTS ABOUT MEN'S DRESS: Right Principles Economically Applied. By a NEW YORK CLUBMAN. 18mo. Parchment-paper, 30 cents.

A useful manual, especially for young men desirous of dressing economically and yet according to the canons of good taste.

New York: D. APPLETON & CO., 72 Fifth Avenue.

GEORGE H. ELLWANGER'S BOOKS.

THE GARDEN'S STORY; or, Pleasures and Trials of an Amateur Gardener. With Head and Tail Pieces by Rhead. 16mo. Cloth, extra, $1.50.

"This dainty nugget of horticultural lore treats of the pleasures and trials of an amateur gardener. From the time when daffodils begin to peer and the 'secret of the year' comes in to mid-October, Mr. Ellwanger provides an outline of hardy flower-gardening that can be carried on and worked upon by amateurs. . . ."—*Philadelphia Public Ledger.*

"One of the most charming books of the season. . . . It is in no sense a text-book, but it combines a vast deal of information with a great deal of out-of-door observation, and exceedingly pleasant and sympathetic writing about flowers and plants."—*Christian Union.*

"A dainty, learned, charming, and delightful book."—*New York Sun.*

THE STORY OF MY HOUSE. With an Etched Frontispiece by Sidney L. Smith, and numerous Head and Tail Pieces by W. C. Greenough. 16mo. Cloth, extra, $1.50.

"An essay on the building of a house, with all its kaleidoscopic possibilities in the way of reform, and its tantalizing successes before the fact, is always interesting; and the author is not niggardly in the good points he means to secure. . . . The book aims only to be agreeable; its literary flavor is pervasive, its sentiment kept well in hand."—*New York Evening Post.*

"When the really perfect book of its class comes to a critic's hands, all the words he has used to describe fairly satisfactory ones are inadequate for his new purpose, and he feels inclined, as in this case, to stand aside and let the book speak for itself. In its own way, it would be hardly possible for this daintily printed volume to do better."—*Art Amateur.*

IN GOLD AND SILVER. With Illustrations by W. Hamilton Gibson, A. B. Wenzell, and W. C. Greenough. 16mo. Cloth, $2.00. Also, limited *édition de luxe*, on Japanese vellum, $5.00.

CONTENTS : The Golden Rug of Kermanshâh; Warders of the Woods; A Shadow upon the Pool; The Silver Fox of Hunt's Hollow.

"After spending a half-hour with 'In Gold and Silver,' one recalls the old saying, 'Precious things come in small parcels.'"—*Christian Intelligencer.*

"One of the handsomest gift-books of the year."—*Philadelphia Inquirer.*

"The whole book is eminently interesting, and emphatically deserving of the very handsome and artistic setting it has received."—*New York Tribune.*

New York : D. APPLETON & CO., 72 Fifth Avenue.

www.ingramcontent.com/pod-product-compliance
Lightning Source LLC
Chambersburg PA
CBHW020540270326
41927CB00006B/664